I Hear America Singing

Walt Whitman

I hear America singing, the varied carols I hear,
Those of mechanics, each one singing his as it should be blithe
    and strong,
The carpenter singing his as he measures his plank or beam,
The mason singing his as he makes ready for work, or leaves
    off work,
The boatman singing what belongs to him in his boat, the
    deck-hand singing on the steamboat deck,
The shoemaker singing as he sits on his bench, the hatter
    singing as he stands,
The wood-cutter's song, the ploughboy's on his way in the
    morning, or at noon intermission or at sundown,
The delicious singing of the mother, or of the young wife at
    work, or of the girl sewing or washing,
Each singing what belongs to him or her and to none else,
The day what belongs to the day—at night the party of young
    fellows, robust, friendly,
Singing with open mouths their strong melodious songs.

When Walt Whitman envisioned an America that was both rich in diversity and yet unified by people working together, he "heard America singing." For when people raise their voices in song, their varied voices support, reinforce, and enliven each other. Each gains strength from the others as they join in cooperation for a common goal. Choral singing is, as Whitman saw, an apt metaphor for the democratic process in which each voice has a role and must be heard. But it is more than a metaphor, for studies have shown that communities that engage in cooperative activities such as choral singing really are more vital and sustaining than those that do not.

"Let freedom ring!"

A chorus of voices—all individual, all distinctive,

but joined in a common effort.

When singers of the Northwest Girlchoir of Seattle

lift their strong voices in song, they celebrate

the hope of a joyous living democracy.

And keep alive the true promise of America,

"sweet land of liberty."

COMPANION TO THE MAJOR PBS SERIES

THE AMERICAN PROMISE

Adventures in Grass-Roots Democracy

JAMES C. CRIMMINS

EDITED BY CAROL AND THOMAS CHRISTENSEN
INTRODUCTION BY STUDS TERKEL
AFTERWORD BY MAXINE HONG KINGSTON

PUBLIC TELEVISION PRODUCTION OF *THE AMERICAN PROMISE* IS MADE POSSIBLE BY
FARMERS INSURANCE GROUP OF COMPANIES

KQED
BOOKS
SAN FRANCISCO

KQED Books & Tapes, 2601 Mariposa St., San Francisco, CA 94110.

VICE PRESIDENT FOR PUBLISHING & NEW VENTURES: Mark K. Powelson
PUBLISHER: Pamela Byers

PROJECT EDITORS: Thomas and Carol Christensen
BOOK AND COVER DESIGN: Paula Schlosser
PHOTO ASSIGNMENT EDITOR: Louise Kollenbaum
PRODUCTION: Penn & Ink / Hong Kong
TEXT COMPOSITION: Harrington-Young Typography & Design
RESEARCH ASSISTANCE: Katy Kennedy, Deborah Hudson, Suzanne Hogan
WRITING ASSISTANCE: Jonathan Halperin, Toody Healy
PRODUCTION ASSISTANCE: Dayna Goforth
STUDS TERKEL INTERVIEW: Paul Loeb

KQED PRESIDENT & CEO: Mary G. F. Bitterman

Principal photography by David Barry, Andrew Eccles, Arlene Gottfried, and Ferne Pearlstein. Complete photo credits will be found on page 197. Text permissions and credits will be found on page 196, which constitutes an extension of this copyright page.

Educational and non-profit groups wishing to order this book at attractive quantity discounts may contact KQED Books & Tapes, 2601 Mariposa St., San Francisco, CA 94110.

LIBRARY OF CONGRESS CATALOGING-IN-PUBLICATION DATA
Crimmins, James C.
 The American promise : adventures in grass-roots democracy/James
C. Crimmins : edited by Carol and Thomas Christensen.
      p.   cm.
   "Companion to the major PBS series."
   Includes bibliographical references.
   ISBN 0-912333-71-5 (pbk.).—ISBN 0-912333-72-3 (hardcover)
   1. Local government—United States. 2. Political participation—
United States. I. American promise (Television program)
II. Title.
JS335.C78   1995
323'.042'0973—dc20   95-37518
                                                          CIP

ISBN 0-912333-71-5 (paperback)
ISBN 0-912333-72-3 (hardcover)

10 9 8 7 6 5 4 3 2

ON FRONT, CLOCKWISE FROM LEFT: Ernesto and Tomás Montoya (photograph by Ferne Pearlstein), John Thompson and son Jason Rogers-Thompson (Chris Shorten), Northwest Girlchoir members (Arlene Gottfried), Spencer Owyang with his wife and children (Ferne Pearlstein).

Distributed to the trade by Publishers Group West

A Letter from the Chairman of the Farmers Insurance Group of Companies

THERE IS NO MORE IMPORTANT TASK before this nation than educating and encouraging citizens. Democracy is a fragile, clumsy, and messy process; it doesn't happen by itself. It is a tough way to run anything, much less a nation. It doesn't come with easy-to-follow instructions or guarantees. But it does give each and every one of us a chance to be heard, an opportunity to change and amend what we don't like and suggest what we think should be done. It thrives when any of us participates and soars when we work together.

We hear a great deal about gridlock in our capitols, about a divided and intolerant society, and a nation too quick to blame. That is a far-from-complete or accurate picture of this country. Out beyond the televised press conferences is an America that is remaking itself daily, changing what has to be changed, finding answers that all of us can use. But, *The American Promise* is not just about hope; it deals with how the system works and how we can work it. It looks at what distinguishes our democracy and makes it something in which we can take pride.

The stories in the series and in this book—from mountain climbing to lobster fishing, from infighting on a rafting trip to revival in tough urban neighborhoods, from volunteers to entrepreneurs, from helpers to those who need help—will make you want to cheer. People in this country are extraordinary. You'll meet more than two hundred of them, none of whom set out to be "citizens" or anything special. One step just led to another.

Democracy is always an unfinished business, subject to change and amendment, and vital because it is so. It takes participation and care to make it work, tolerance and a collective belief in the future to make it thrive.

At Farmers, we have always believed in helping communities and thus agreed to underwrite the project from its start. It took three years to complete. Working with a distinguished board of academic, community, and education advisors, the producers have scoured this country to capture who and what makes our democracy work, rediscovering the strength and power of our system.

Certainly, we do not believe that a three-hour series like this book and teaching guides that will accompany it in communities and schools—will solve the nation's problems, but it will help equip those who have to solve them.

It is with pride in our democracy, in the people of Farmers Insurance who are committed to helping their communities, and in a project that I think can make a difference for all of us, that we made possible *The American Promise*.

—LEO DENLEA

CONTENTS

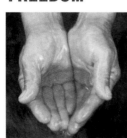

PREFACE

THE FIRST PROMISE OF DEMOCRACY is freedom. Our most important freedom is the freedom to question, to ask *why?*

The question that led to this book and the companion PBS series was, Why did our democracy seem to be failing us—even though the rest of the world was rushing to copy it? The evening newscasts were full of injustice, intolerance, division, violence. Call-in radio and talk shows had turned exchanges of the day into therapy—a nation of pioneers started to look like a nation of victims. We were looking backward for someone to blame, not forward to the future. Polls tapped into our private prejudices by asking how we felt, not what we thought. Feel words started to outnumber thought words in the front pages of even our best newspapers, substituting contempt for contemplation, insinuation for information. We were at home on the couch. A battalion of pleaders and pullers tugged at our democracy at various points of power, and we seemed helpless to do anything but "throw the bums out" every few years.

Politics, with all of its shaded meanings, had driven us to the sidelines—few of us like going to town meetings, out of fear of offending neighbors, of making fools of ourselves, or of speaking out in public. (As one wag noted, most of us would rather be the subject of an eulogy than the one to deliver it.) Fewer of us were anxious to encounter the absolutism of protest groups. Deliberation and debate had been replaced by debunking. Motives were questioned, opponents maligned, losers trashed. Factionalism ruled. Shouting was the key to the new form of democracy. It was our rational wisdom (or what political scientists perversely call "rational ignorance") to stay home, unsullied. What difference could any of us make? One vote? One voice? What we seemed to have on our hands was a loss of faith in ourselves and our democratic system. Our national problems were growing bigger and more complicated daily. Even with so much at stake, voter turnout seemed to drop

A horse of a different color. The citizens of Missoula, Montana, found new ways of working together to create a community-built carousel.

further every November, while public debate centered on personalities, not issues. The rest of the world is trying to copy us. Are they crazy?

Despite the nightly news diet of tragedy and tears, despite the litany of problems and postponed answers, when we began this project we reasoned that somewhere the system must be working. We keep changing it—a sure sign of democratic faith. Beyond the media glare at the center and the push–pull of the spin doctors and pundits, there must be a place where the system of citizen rule serves the citizens.

"The job can only be done by citizens who work together in a community."

So began a three-year journey of questions: How and why does our democracy work, under what conditions does it thrive? More than a dozen researchers and field producers joined the hunt for working democracies, for grass-roots heroes who make our democracy work and show us how to work it. We started by reading newspapers from cities and towns, large and small, all over the country; meeting with the first recruits for our distinguished board of advisors and networking amongst citizen groups.

In the months that followed, the team found hundreds of examples of dynamic grass-root democracy. We found conflict, the sure stuff of drama. We also found quiet talk and the silence of careful listening. We found the friction that is generated by facing hard choices when cultures, backgrounds, identities, and values clash. It is what makes us dynamic and adaptable. We have to make hard choices in order to go forward.

We found blacksmiths and bankers, ambulance drivers and ranchers, Eskimo elders and street artists, homemakers and students who were enjoying the full power of being citizens and using that power to reshape their lives and their communities.

Some observers were quick to remind us that individual citizens just did not matter, that any little thing or two grass-roots activists might accomplish was so much "spitting in the wind." Small victories do not matter. The game was played where the bigger boys played and kept score in billions.

These cynics' challenges are answered best by the people you will read about in this book. In hundreds of communities across this country we found people finding new ways to work together to build and rebuild communities, to interact with each other and with the government in order to make a difference.

Good citizens make good neighborhoods and good cities. A good representative on a city council or in the state legislature or in Congress can bring resources to a city, but she or he cannot make it a good city. That job can only be done by citizens who work together in a community group or chorus to build the underlying web of trust and commitment that creates what is called *social capital*—the collective value of a community's wealth. Advisor Robert D. Putnam's work made us conscious of how critical social capital is and how people push it into place. Pour economic capital into a community with little or no social capital and it disappears like water on sand. Pour money into a thriving, active community and it generates a return, multiplies possibilities.

WITH A LIBRARY OF STORIES under our belts, our panel of twenty-one educator, academic, and community-leader advisors worked together to define the underlying factors that truly make a democracy work. After a good many sessions and much debate, the factors were boiled down to nine, grouped into bunches of three. Then we tested the terms in the classroom. High school students called the nine "the language of democracy." This language provides the structure for this book and the PBS series.

The language includes the touchstones any democracy must have to operate: *freedom, responsibility,* and *participation. Freedom* is choice—to take chances. The freedom to fail and try again, gives a democracy a growth dimension. Getting it right the first time, every time works only for dictators, and then only because they say it is "right." *Responsibility,* the flip side of rights, is what is expected of us, in a society where we are the rulers. *Participation* is the air democracy breathes. If we citizens stay home, who is minding the democracy? It is ours to make of it whatever we can. And, if we don't, to paraphrase George Bernard Shaw, "We get the democracy we deserve."

In the second set of three are the factors that operate a democracy. A democracy has to have good *information.* Each of us has to know what is truly happening if our actions are to be effective. We have to be able to sift what is information from speculation, news from sound-bite quips and trial balloons. The pressure is on us as much as upon the media. A democracy also requires *deliberation.* We have to gather together and, recognizing each other's positions, work out solutions. This requires a thoughtful not just a forceful interchange. Competing arguments must be heard. Then there are *hard choices.* We must face our differences honestly. Making the tough decisions makes us dynamic and adaptable; it forges us into communities.

The third and last threesome: *opportunity, leverage,* and *common ground.* We have to understand how to use opportunity, find leverage so that our voices can be heard, and find common ground so that with others we can build communities. We can make differences when we believe we can. *Opportunity* is will, persistence—coming back for another try. *Leverage* is finding what we have nearby by that we can use to create not noise, but change. Home runs start at home. *Common ground* is about having differences, but valuing the result of common purpose.

THREE YEARS OF RESEARCH have shown us two Americas. While we have found great innovation and vitality at the grass roots, as a nation we seem to have found the brakes. One complaint, in an over-sensitized political arena, is too many. Anyone can stop anything anytime. We have forgotten that democracy is conflict, that we all have different values, beliefs, backgrounds, experiences, outlooks. We need to talk, deliberate, find new ways to deal with our problems. To set and reset what we are about so that each of us has the freedoms we need.

Our conclusion was that the country perceived politics as a game show where the contestants won, but not the viewers. It came with usual self-congratulatory hype, annoying commercials, cued applause, popularity ratings, and told us nothing of the world outside the game. We changed channels. Politics was no longer perceived as the larger process by which we govern ourselves—which is a tragedy because each of us has better expectations for our society, if not for ourselves, then as a citizen. Perhaps this is because for the most part all we see of politics is on television.

Democracy is alive and well at the grass roots. Does this matter? It matters a great deal. The new science of "complexity" shows that complex interactive organisms—like a democracy—stay healthy and thrive by changing at the margin, not at the center. The work of the Santa Fe Institute focuses on complexity. Its faculty of Nobel Laureates and leading-edge thinkers has studied complex, adaptive systems such as democracies, economies, stock markets, cultures, computers, and the human brain. They have found that hierarchical systems are too slow in reacting to and accommodating change, and thus sooner or later are rendered useless. Doyne Farmer, a member of the Institute, said "It is pretty clear that the totalitarian, centralized approach to the organization of society doesn't work very well. Evolution thrives in systems with bottom-up organization which gives rise to flexibility."

"Hard won answers to real problems are forged by the acts of citizen volunteers."

Real change happens at the grass roots. Change comes slowly in our capitols, and then only reluctantly, for bureaucratic forces there tend to preserve the status quo, to keep us on an even keel. They are, oftentimes, distant from our problems or needs. We are the best judge of these.

Democracy as we found it is not an idea; it is an activity. At the grass roots, answers are not in statistics or think-tank papers, they are in working, hard-won answers to real problems. They are forged by the acts of citizen volunteers who somehow make it their jobs to get involved, to make democracy work. This is not to say that grass-roots democracy is paradise or panacea. None of the answers created by citizen volunteers are necessarily the answers. Answers come and go. The process— and its problems, some old, some new—endure.

Our last task was a title. We had started out referring to what we sought as "the American process." But *process* lacks the people dimension. Along the way we discovered that the earliest settlers in their town meetings in the 1600s had no set of rules to guide them, only a promise made out loud to work together. This common trust or promise was extended to the *Declaration of Independence,* which was very much a promissory note as the founders pledged their "lives, fortunes, and sacred honor." So we called the series *The American Promise,* not because of the promises shining or otherwise that are said to be inherent to our society, but because democracy is a promise each of us has to keep.

Democracy is a leap of faith we have to make. In this project, that first leap was made by Farmers Insurance Group of Companies and its chairman, Leo Denlea. If Farmers had not made a leap of trust, investing in this project, exhibiting extraordinary citizenship, the PBS series would not have happened.

A democracy is a summary of our hopes, problems, realities, and possibilities at a given time—all subject to revision tomorrow. It is constant change, amendment, adaptation that keeps any democracy alive. Democracy is an unfinished journey. It has its bumps and pot holes. But, when it works, giving room for its citizens to reinvent and reinvigorate it, it thrives as no other system can. We invite you to share our rediscovery of our democracy and the people in whose care it remains.

JAMES C. CRIMMINS
Atherton, California
1995

INTRODUCTION

An Interview with Studs Terkel

In August, 1995, author Studs Terkel met in Chicago to discuss The American Promise *with Paul Loeb, author of* Generation at the Crossroads: Apathy and Action on the American Campus. *Their conversation ranged between the particular stories and the larger themes they raise. Terkel spoke with passion about his vision for America. His inspiring and provocative comments, recorded by Loeb, are reproduced here.*

SOMETHING HAPPENED TO THE PEOPLE in this book, these individuals who took part for maybe the first time in their lives. They are not the same people anymore. Even if they lost the fight, they won something else—a sense of community.

Right now there is no one national cause. There is no coalescence around huge issues, such as the civil rights movement of the sixties or the anti-war movement. But there are many community groups and action groups, as *The American Promise* demonstrates.

We are talking about two aspects of America. Two currents, one against the other. There is the communitarian aspect—the community—against the dog-eat-dog aspect. The dog-eat-dog aspect is the one that seems to be winning. But this book shows that there are also many community groups around and about the country.

We are told today to be competitive: every man for himself. Competition has become the *modus vivendi*. Watch a TV commercial for ghetto kids, black kids or poor white kids: "Go to school because competition's the big thing. You can learn to compete." Is that why we go to school? To learn to compete in the world? Or to enrich ourselves as people and thus enrich the community? Competition means beating somebody else, and as long as that is the case, we are in a rough situation, because more are going to lose than win. That is why you have billionaires increasing in number, and why the gap between the haves and have-nots is greater than ever, too. Fewer and fewer people have more and more power—thus more and more dough. And more and more people have less.

Most of us think of the American dream as the idea of approaching a new world where there will be a new chance in the race of life. Of those who came voluntarily, many came to escape the conscription that was pervasive everywhere. Most of them came to make a living, to put bread on the table. The dream means a better chance. To quote Lincoln, "Everyone is entitled to a fair chance in the race of life."

Of course, there were also the involuntary immigrants, kidnapped off the coast of West Africa. To them the Statue of Liberty looks different. In my book *The Great Divide,* Maggie Holmes, a black domestic worker, says that passing the Statue of Liberty "doesn't mean to me what it means to you."

The twist in the American dream is that you come across so many kids who are lost and bewildered, and what they say is "I'm not going to be as well-off as my old man." Their ancestors came seeking bread on the table. They were looking for freedom from hunger, freedom from privation. How can you even talk about freedom if people are hungry and starving?

> **"We say 'American dream' but it is a universal dream. Throughout all epochs there have been people interested in community."**

But part of the American dream was community. We say "American dream" but it is a universal dream. Throughout all epochs there have been people interested in community and protesting. Were it not for those we call "flakes"—subversives and rebels—there might be no human species alive today.

Take the Roman Empire—in power through violence. Along comes a subversive group headed by a guy named Christ. Who is this agitator named Christ? He has a philosophy that is subversive. He says, "Love thy neighbor." What is that stuff, love thy neighbor? The whole idea is "Beat up thy neighbor." And along comes this guy with the subversive doctrine.

In America we think of the abolitionists, who took a hell of a beating. Or woman suffragists, the early ones. People always challenging, whether it be slavery or whether it be the big boys. Whether it be the Workers' Alliance, something left-wing back in the thirties, or whether it be different groups helping in our time, fighting pollution. There are many examples in this book.

People think they lose individuality if they belong to a community group. But the opposite is true. You become stronger as an individual. Einstein said that when you become part of something, your own individuality is there as you speak out, far more than if you are alone. When a person becomes involved as part of a community, the juices start flowing.

WHEN I WAS GROWING UP, my folks had a hotel, a men's hotel, where working men lived. It was a good hotel during the twenties, all the rooms full. Then came the Depression. You'd find the guys in the lobby more and more, arguing and getting drunk and fighting.

But the hotel was always full of argument. See, back in those days, working men *read*. Not all, but far more than today. They read their Little Blue Books. Did you ever hear of E. Haldeman-Julius' Blue Books? They were little books that people would subscribe to. They cost a nickel or a dime. It could be Clarence Darrow on the hereafter, Tom Paine's *Age of Reason,* Voltaire. They had everything. They had the plays of Shakespeare for ten cents. In books little enough that you could fit them right in your shirt pocket.

It was a minority who read, but a good minority. And they always argued, in the hotel lobby. But today, the average ordinary person comes home, he's tired, and he has TV. Who runs TV? A new conglomerate has just come into being, a new monopoly, ABC and Disney. It's simply par for the course. Fewer and fewer control more and more.

Recapturing our history is part of our job. But how do you recapture a history, if history itself is distorted day after day after day? More than distorted, it is buried. There is no yesterday. As we watch television, news is fused with entertainment: one becomes the other. Whether it is sports or entertainment, what is news? "Entertainment Tonight" is news. Something happens to us: memory, the events that passed, they are no longer there. In other words, we are at this moment suffering what I call a national Alzheimer's disease. There is no memory of what happened a moment ago. That is the stacked deck we're playing against.

It's a tough battle. Since you don't control the media, you try to get as much of a voice in as you can. Through community groups, on some issue that is popular, like stopping pollution or a developer in the area...it can be a very local issue, very localized indeed. The way to beat the stacked deck is in these groups, with people who start with a local issue. Whether it is about little kids in a project here, or lobster fishermen, or that little Hispanic woman who stopped Waste Management trucks from dumping stuff in her area. Or Mary Lou Wolff, who lives on the northwest side of Chicago. A conservative, Mary Lou finds out the city is going to build an expressway right through her area. And Mary Lou gets up and says, "Who needs this expressway?" And the group called CAP started when they won the fight. They became the Committee Against Pollution. And then the Citizens Action Program.

That leads to something else on the part of the person involved. The community groups *The American Promise* is talking about are all-important; not simply for their individual fights, but for what it leads the person who takes part in them for the first time to see over and beyond that. It reminds me of the old Chinese poem that begins, "I work in the community," and then the neighborhood, and then the city, and then the country, and then the world, and it all begins with me. That's how it ends. "And it all begins with me." In that little community.

Because there is no one national cause, things are diffuse at the moment. But something else has happened that has affected our country for the worse. That is the "counter-revolution" with its "trickle-down" theory. Help the big boys because the money, the good, will trickle down elsewhere. It didn't, we know that. Something else trickled down—the mean-spiritedness of that movement trickled down. It is the old routine of divide and conquer. It is the perversion of the American dream.

What gives me hope? Let's put it this way. I have hope, but I'm not an optimist. "Hope dies last." I got that saying from Jessie de la Cruz. She's in my book *American Dreams: Lost and Found*, the woman who joined the farm workers union of Cesar Chavez and started speaking out, demanding the growers pay a decent wage. She said, "Is America progressing toward the better? No, the country will never do anything for us. We are the ones that are going to do it. We have to keep on struggling. I feel there's going to be a change. With us there's a saying: *La esperanza muere el último.* Hope dies last. You can't lose hope. If you lose hope, that's losing everything."

Nothing is perfectible about men and women, the human species. The same species that wrote *Hamlet,* and *The Marriage of Figaro,* and the *Ninth Symphony,* also did Auschwitz and Hiroshima. Same species. So it depends what the society you are in values the most. The dream was always to make a buck or two, I suppose. It hasn't changed to that extent, but what has changed is the nature of indifference.

There's a phrase Jacob Bronowsky, the British physicist and man of letters used. He was in a plane over Nagasaki. He saw the rubble that was there after the bombing. And he said, "It's not that man's indifference to man has changed; it's the scale of the indifference." The scale is so huge because of technology. We can knock off a million at a time now.

> **"People think they lose individuality if they belong to a community group. But the opposite is true. You become stronger as an individual when you become part of something."**

We come back to community versus the competitive air that we have today. As I said, something happens to the people described in this book, *The American Promise,* when they fight. They are not the same people anymore. They scared that group, that big guy, that Goliath. "I never dreamed I could do that!" so many say. Why not ask these people about hope?

Like Nancy Jefferson, who died recently. She is in *American Dreams.* She said, "Down in the country, we used to have to ring the bell if there was trouble or we'd ring it for dinner. We used to pull this rope. Sometimes, especially if it was cold, you'd keep pulling and keep pulling the bell. You'd think you'd never hear a sound. Maybe by the time your hands got raw almost, you'd hear a little tinkling of the bell. That's the way I visualize the community. We all keep pulling at the rope and our hands are getting raw, but you do hear a little tinkling. We have got to do it. We must do it. We have no choice. We have got to keep pulling, and I believe the bell will ring."

And I say that I believe it, too. Ask the people in this book.

"This is my country!" The American *Promise* PBS series (and accompanying compact disk) features many choral numbers, both old and new. The Moses Hogan Chorale of New Orleans performs Hogan's arrangement of Ed Bogas's music for Langston Hughes's "Let America Be America Again," a bittersweet poem giving voice to the hopes of African-Americans. The Chorale also sings "Grass Roots" and "The Promise," original compositions celebrating democracy.

The Chorale is going on tour with songs from *The American Promise,* as well as traditional spirituals and blues—songs that paint a musical portrait of this country's desires and dreams.

The American Promise
By James C. Crimmins

We made a promise and we signed our
    names.
We pledged our honor and our lives.
It was our country to do with whatever
    we could.
It was a promise that we made to each
    other,
Of the people, by the people, for the
    people.
We made a promise to ourselves and
    each other
And we signed our names.

To work together, to trust each other—
Trust is the ink in which we sign our
    names.
Will it still be there when we sign our
    names?
Will it still be there when we sign our
    names?

"Let America be America Again":

The Langston Hughes poem is brought to life by the Moses Hogan Chorale

"I hear

Part One

America

Of the People

singing,

FREEDOM

the varied

RESPONSIBILITY

carols

PARTICIPATION

I hear..."

> "Democracy is based upon the conviction that there are extraordinary possibilities in ordinary people."
>
> —Henry Emerson Fosdick

DEMOCRACY IS BOTH AN IDEAL and the quest for that ideal. It is an adventure, a covenant we make with ourselves and with each other, a promise we keep for the generations to follow. To keep the ideal alive, we must shift attention from politicians to ordinary people who are working with one another to build communities.

The evening news dwells on the big event, the great conflict, the spectacular failure. It focuses on the center and magnifies even the smallest events there, mistaking urgency for importance. But in thousands of communities, away from the glare of the media, hidden from the scrutiny of pundits, democracy is working today—because citizens are making it work.

Every generation, and every citizen, wrestles with the innate dilemmas of democracy: Who represents me, and how well am I represented? What difference does my one vote—or my one voice—make in a nation of millions? When values clash, what is fair, and who decides? What do we, the people, hold in common? What does the majority owe to the minority? How can we prevent the tyranny of the many over the few? Or of the few over the many?

"Optimists may believe that democracy is the inevitable and final form of human society, but the historical record shows that up to now it has been the rare exception." For democracy to flourish, a society must **"have a body of citizens who possess a good understanding of the principles of democracy, or who at least have developed a character consistent with the democratic way of life."**

—Donald Kagan, *Pericles of Athens and the Birth of Democracy*

Democratic government can never be a finished system, for it is, as William H. Hastie observed, "a process, not a static condition. It is becoming, rather than being. It can be easily lost, but is never finally won." It is always a summary of who and what we are at a particular time; an accumulation of our fears, hopes, beliefs, and needs; a collection of possibilities. It is subject to and, indeed, *dependent* upon constant change and amendment.

Ask an American what democracy means and a common answer is "freedom." But our idea of unlimited freedom must confront the real limits of the world's resources.

One model for thinking about the fair use of shared resources is "the theory of the commons," based on a traditional English village. A *commons* is property held in common—an open meadow that can be used by any villager to pasture cattle. William Forster Lloyd, the mathematically trained Oxford don who first proposed the theory in 1883, reached a conclusion that should be familiar to any student of human behavior. If there is nothing to prevent a greedy villager from overusing the shared resources, the rewards or profits would go to the greedy herdsman. But the losses caused by depleting the resources would be shared by the entire community.

This theory has been used to justify regulation of a free market economy. Garrett Hardin has turned the theory into a powerful—and controversial—argument against overpopulation. But Hardin also uses it as a defense of small communities that are able to achieve a self-regulated balance and meet the needs of all the people in the community.

Democracy does not come with easy-to-follow instructions, or a lifetime guarantee. The system is inefficient and requires a lot of maintenance. Running it is a messy and difficult—but vital—process.

"No one pretends that democracy is perfect or all-wise," Winston Churchill remarked. "Democracy is the worst form of government except all those other forms that have been tried from time to time."

The stakes are high . . .

Who Says I Can't?

"OUR LIVES, OUR FORTUNES, and our sacred honor" are on the line—so said the signers of the *Declaration of Independence*. The founders of our country risked everything for freedom. Thanks to them, we Americans enjoy great personal freedoms and individual rights.

"It's a free country," we say. We are free to reinvent government, to build our businesses, to raise our children, to speak our minds. We value our freedom of choice—the freedom to express ourselves, to consume, and to experience.

But it takes ordinary citizens putting their hands in the air, questioning and challenging, to keep our freedoms alive and well. The battles fought by the founders of our nation are not and will never be finished; it is up to us to continue the fight.

We can still learn from the founders' struggles. In the late 1700s, as American resentment of British rule was growing, grand new notions of individual freedom and human rights were in the air. As John Adams later observed, "the Revolution was effected before the war commenced. The Revolution was in the minds and hearts of the people.... This radical change in the principles, opinions, and affections of the people was the real American Revolution."

That revolution had actually begun in Europe. In the 1760s, Jean-Jacques Rousseau had lamented, "Man is born free, but everywhere he is enslaved." Soon his countrymen Diderot, Montesquieu, and Voltaire were among the many advocating a new philosophy of individual liberty. At the end of the century, after Americans such as Benjamin Franklin and Thomas

. . . the precious blessings of freedom

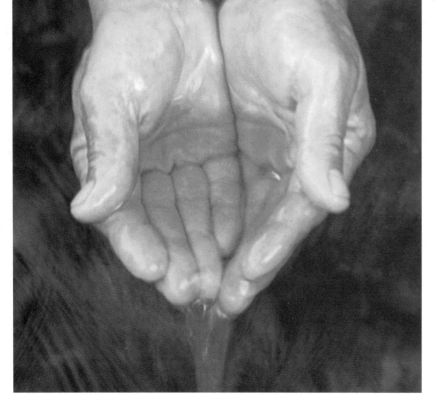

Jefferson had developed and refined the French philosophers' ideas and had put them into action, those ideas culminated in the French Revolution. Jefferson suggested that individual freedoms would flourish when the powers of the state were constantly questioned. "I like a little rebellion now and then," he wrote. "The spirit of rebellion to government is so valuable on occasion that I wish it to be always kept alive." Thus, the message of freedom had crossed the ocean only to return and refresh its source.

In April of 1773, Jefferson, together with Patrick Henry, Richard Henry Lee, Francis Lightfoot Lee, and Dabney Carr (all members of the British colonial government in Virginia), formed what they called a "Committee of Correspondence." The Committee was charged with defending citizen's rights. An informal network of like-minded Americans was set up to share information among the colonies and "produce a unity of action." From this network for exchanging information and expressing ideas and opinions, new concepts of human rights emerged that culminated three years later in Jefferson's *Declaration of Independence*. As Merrill D. Peterson put it, "A revolution of the mind became the basis of a revolution of government."

"The republic," said Carl Sandburg, "is a dream." Can individual rights without individual responsibilities produce a nightmare? What does freedom mean in social terms? The clash between freedom and limits is one of the persistent dilemmas

Some fear that Americans have come to the same pass as Athenians at the end of the Golden Age of Greek democracy. As Edward Gibbon described their decline,

"**More than they wanted freedom, they wanted security. When the Athenians wanted not to give to society, but society to give to them, when the freedom they wished for was the freedom from responsibility, then Athens ceased to be free.**"

"Thomas Jefferson was a great democrat and a great apostle of freedom, but if he came back from the dead today, the range of choices would amaze and no doubt horrify him—choices people are allowed and encouraged to make in every walk of life, all in the name of freedom: choices about sexual and family relationships, about religious identity, about ways of talking, dressing, acting, and so on.

"From our contemporary viewpoint, the scope of individualism was more limited in the nineteenth century. Theorists (and perhaps the majority of the population) certainly celebrated freedom, democracy, and popular sovereignty. And, of course, their concept of freedom necessarily implied individual choice, as a central value in social life. Personal autonomy was another value—freedom from outside interference, as well as the right of the individual to develop the self to the fullest, to pursue his or her own goals, to control the conditions of existence.

"All this sounds a great deal like the modern form; but the definition implied in actual practice was subtly different. Theory and practice defined freedom primarily in political or economic terms—in terms of markets and votes. Those who spoke about development of self were thinking of a self quite unlike its twentieth-century descendant. It was a God-fearing, hard-working, disciplined, traditional self, as far as private life was concerned."

—LAWRENCE M. FRIEDMAN, *THE REPUBLIC OF CHOICE: LAW, AUTHORITY, AND CULTURE*

of any democracy. What are the limits of individual freedom, and who sets them? Can a limit be fair to both the individual and the community? Can an understanding of limits inspire new solutions to social problems?

Freedom's achievement must be to forge common bonds, a common purpose. We must learn what Alexis de Tocqueville called the "habits of the democratic heart," the balance between individual concerns and collective thought and action.

Dwindling resources and the fight for survival:

"There may be no business in Maine that is more a symbol of our state," agreed participants at a 1993 hearing on lobster fishing. In fact, Maine provides 71% of the entire lobster catch for the Atlantic coast.

"Lobster fishing is hard and sometimes dangerous work. But it is one of the few jobs where a person can truly be their own boss," said Senator Cohen.

"It is a trade that in many cases is still passed down from one generation to the next. As such it is a tradition and a way

of life that those of us who live in Maine want to protect."

Traditionally lobstermen run their own businesses. A few men, sometimes a man and a woman, go out on small wooden boats, equipped with their own traps and lines, and fish within agreed-upon territories. They take as many lobsters as the law allows but leave undersized lobsters and egg-bearing females to ensure enough of a seed crop for harvest the next year or the next. In what used to be one of the ocean's richest territories

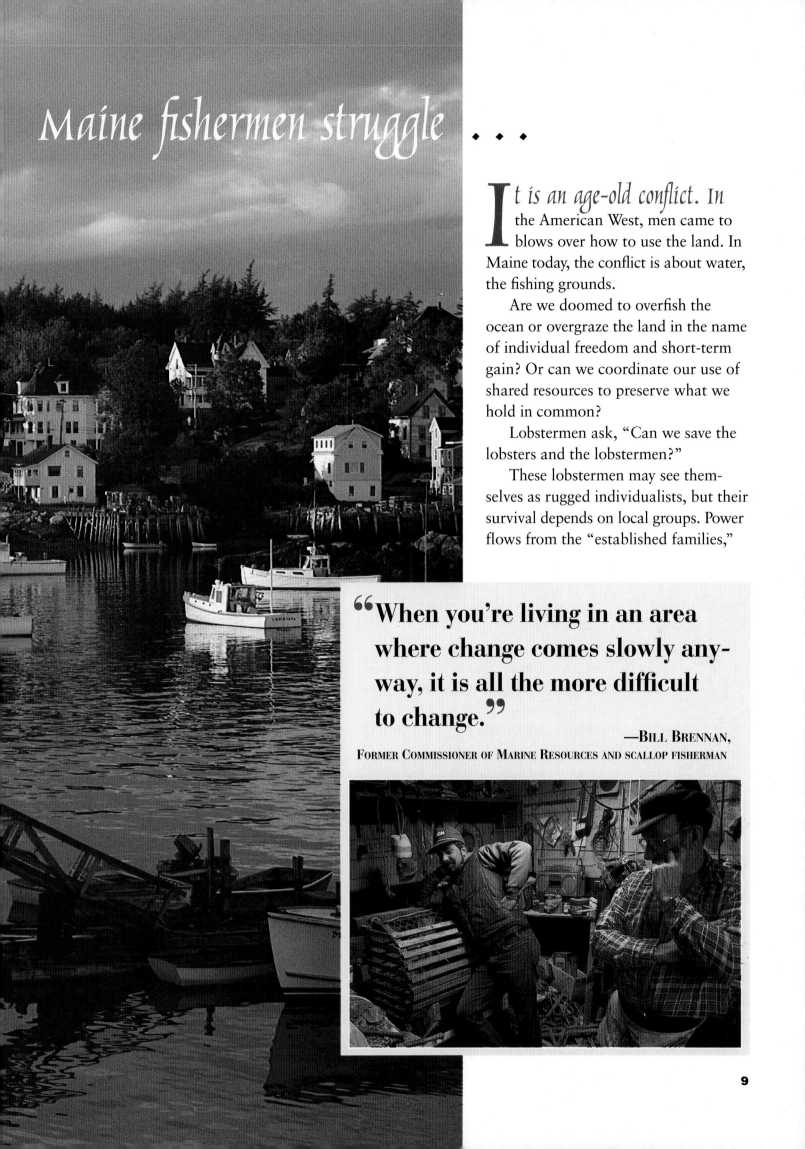

Maine fishermen struggle . . .

It is an age-old conflict. In the American West, men came to blows over how to use the land. In Maine today, the conflict is about water, the fishing grounds.

Are we doomed to overfish the ocean or overgraze the land in the name of individual freedom and short-term gain? Or can we coordinate our use of shared resources to preserve what we hold in common?

Lobstermen ask, "Can we save the lobsters and the lobstermen?"

These lobstermen may see themselves as rugged individualists, but their survival depends on local groups. Power flows from the "established families,"

> "**When you're living in an area where change comes slowly anyway, it is all the more difficult to change.**"
>
> —BILL BRENNAN,
> FORMER COMMISSIONER OF MARINE RESOURCES AND SCALLOP FISHERMAN

. . . to preserve a way of life.

whether they are actual relatives, fishing cooperatives, or harbor gangs. Conflicts are common among "bull" fishermen with established territories, with pressure increased by part-time haulers working day jobs and trying to make a few bucks at night operating tiny skiffs. Competition is acute, territoriality is fierce, and retribution is swift and deliberate. When "two men get to fighting" lobster traps are destroyed, boats sunk, and docks and fish houses burnt. As the number of traps along the coast has increased, with the average lobsterman now operating 1,000 traps, so have disputes over territory. By July 1993, the ocean was at full boil when one Portland group attacked another by ramming their boat, firing weapons, and throwing the gear, and the captain, overboard.

There is another seasonal conflict between lobstermen and scallop fishermen. According to Bill Brennan, former Commissioner of Marine Resources and ex–scallop fisherman, the critical factor in that conflict is "the gear they're using. Lobstermen use what is called fixed gear. They set lobster traps on the bottom affixed to wharves or rope with a buoy on the surface, and they leave that there overnight or longer and go back and harvest the lobster by hauling the trap back. Scallopers use a dredge or a drag and they drag that along the bottom to harvest the scallops.... You tow mobile gear through fixed gear, it destroys it."

Lobstermen want a fair shot at fishing the fertile ground without losing their trap lines to draggers. Scallopers want a chance to fish the bottom without entangling their gear with cumbersome lobster traps. The task of the Maine Marine Resources Department is to establish how best to allow both

"I mean, let's face it, the fisheries really are the last bastion of open range..."
—Bill Brennan

activities to occur at the same place at the same time. "Now there usually isn't a best way to do that," Brennan says.

Draggermen too compete for the ocean's bounty. Lobstermen see drag-fishing crews as the greatest threat to their own livelihood. These fishermen from other New England states drag three miles off the Maine coast, in federal waters, harvesting fish and lobsters that they cannot legally land in Maine. Their heavy nets scour the bottom of traditional lobstering grounds, and

Lobstermen, scallopers, and draggers compete for resources

according to David Cousens, president of the Maine Lobstermen's Association, these "pirates out of Gloucester and New Bedford" return to port with a haul of ground fish, plus seven to eight thousand pound catches of lobsters, including egg-bearing females, which are protected by marine law. "These guys are destroying our future," says Cousens. "They're wrecking the brood stock wholesale. That will hurt us for the next fifty years."

Changes in the fishing industry threaten the tranquility of the bountiful waters off the coast of Maine.

There are 3,500 miles of coast in the state of Maine. Whose ocean is it anyway?

The state has jurisdiction to the three-mile limit. Beyond that is federal water, extended to 200 miles by the Magnuson Act of 1976, which was designed to protect coastal waters from foreign fishing fleets. Yet in the three years following its passage, the number of pounds of fish landed in New England grew by almost 50%. Modern fishing methods—huge metal trawlers replacing the old wooden fishing boats, improved fish-finding technology (sonar, underwater TV cameras, satellite images displayed on computer screens),

gigantic fish-processing ships—have severely depleted major fishing stocks, with cod, flounder and haddock landings in 1989 less than one-fourth of what they had been in the 1960s. Scientists and other analysts have warned that "the worldwide fishing crisis may be too advanced to halt." According to Bill Brennan, the International Lobster Congress "was all about bringing the lobster industry into a realization that they are just one component of a global marketplace for fisheries products... that the days of doing business the way your grandfather did business have changed."

Still, the short-term solutions proposed follow traditional lines: changes in trap limits, time limits, area limits, season limits, size limits, limits on

"...no one can legislate what goes on in the fog off the coast of Maine."

—BILL BRENNAN

sternmen or trap-haulers. Overfishing is to be monitored by a stock-assessment program based on a record-keeping system the lobstermen contend "is going to be something like 800 forms a month."

Lobstermen have expressed tremendous anger against the "federal fish managers" and their "computer models" and "extrapolations"—the "harvest quotas mandated by Washington."

Threatened with tighter federal regulations, lobstermen are working with local and state agencies to find fair solutions for everyone. "As far as the laws of the state are concerned," Bill Brennan insists, "the fishermen do not own the water. We have a public trust responsibility to manage the resources for all of the people of the state."

People in Maine have a tradition of conserving resources, of providing for the future. Everyone in the fishing communities must have a role in crafting new ways of conserving the resources that are the community's lifeblood.

"I'm looking for fairness. These proposals will hurt the little guy. I think we all ought to be treated the same."

"People having their say is the way to go," a lobsterman says, and their voices *are* being heard at public hearings on new regulations. They are joking, arguing, shouting, working together toward self-imposed limits. "There's definitely going to be a point where there's gonna have to be something done. It could be a moratorium or a trap limit or some other means to slow down the harvesting of the resource, but what it's going to be, I really don't know," says one young lobsterman, "just started out in fishing."

"The boats are bigger, the rope is better, the winches are stronger. We're still increasing our yearly catch throughout Maine. But the lobsters are cheaper this year than they've ever been before. Maybe it's just been too good for too long."

The potential for loss to the entire community, the entire region, is enormous. Changes in the natural balance can fundamentally affect the lives of future generations.

In 1994, Georges Bank, once an extraordinarily rich fishing ground, was closed to fishing until the New England Fishery Management Council approves a new set of fishing regulations, probably early in 1996. Federal legislation too is under consideration.

"No *pesce*," complain cod, flounder, and haddock fishermen whose catch last year was the lowest ever recorded, with haddock less than 2% of harvest during the boom 30 years ago. For the many communities that have depended on drag-fishing for centuries, this is a tragedy.

With fishing grounds up and down the Eastern seaboard threatened, lobstermen, scallopers, and draggers are meeting with the state commissioner and with environmental activists. Together they are trying to hammer out a solution to their problems and the problems of Atlantic fisheries.

Private needs and public spaces: anti-graffiti

"**W**e should have the freedom to express ourselves," wall writers insist, as their spray paint and ink "marks" spread across our cities and towns.

"If you want to call it freedom of expression," answers Jane Golden, Director of Murals for the Philadelphia Anti-Graffiti Network, "everybody has their right to expression, but there are also laws, and if you're going to tag another person's property, then you're going to have to suffer the consequences."

When graffiti "taggers" in Philadelphia are enrolled in Golden's unique program, the consequence is public art—and a flowering of community spirit, as community-designed murals spring up on the walls of some of the city's roughest neighborhoods.

"What we try to do is have the young people express themselves, but learn that they need to express themselves within the context. Prior to any mural's beginning, we go out and we meet with the community groups. Together we discuss what should go up there. Because it belongs to them. It is their wall. It is their painting."

"Public art," Golden says, "is a partnership between the artist and the community." This new partnership has had a profound effect on the people it touches. As the anti-graffiti project shows, "Art saves lives."

program leads to community rebirth . . .

"The Children's Garden," "Old Philadelphia," "The Civil Rights Struggle," "Local Heroes." These are just some of the 1,200 murals the anti-graffiti project has created around the city during its 10-year history. There is a waiting list of more than 1,000 people who want the mural project to begin the process of cleaning up and unifying their neighborhoods. When coalitions form to discuss mural site, subject, and style, they often stay together for other community projects.

Making a mural leads to making a garden. The mural near Shared House led to another children's garden for Philadelphia. Vegetable patches, flower gardens, an outdoor soup kitchen, African culture workshops, all have blossomed in the shadow of the murals. Rachel Bagby, who created a neighborhood garden, stands in front of a mural of local kids who worked to earn a place on the wall. The murals, says Tim Spencer, Director, are so inspiring they would bring hope, even in "hell country."

. . . *as artists explore freedom and limits.*

The neighborhood mural "is something that reflects the energy of the young people and their desires," Jane Golden explains. "It's a place where these young people have made their mark." The program has taken away their spray paint, and "given them other tools to make their statement." Those tools have led to a lot of success stories: GED exams passed, businesses started, new self-esteem.

"Getting to paint" is a long process even after a neighborhood agrees on a subject. Putting up scaffolding, scrubbing and whitewashing the wall, gridding, sketching, coloring, and sealing are all part of the team process of creating a mural. Network kids start out on these jobs, working their way up through the ranks to assume lead-artist responsibilities.

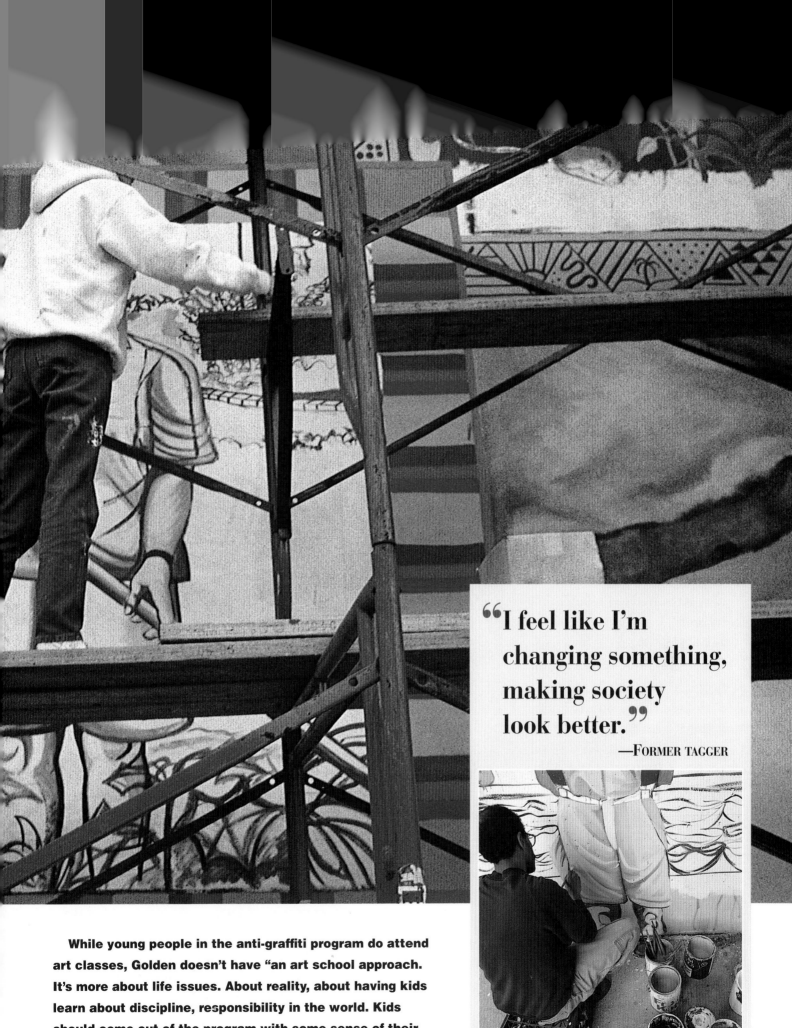

> "I feel like I'm changing something, making society look better."
>
> —FORMER TAGGER

While young people in the anti-graffiti program do attend art classes, Golden doesn't have "an art school approach. It's more about life issues. About reality, about having kids learn about discipline, responsibility in the world. Kids should come out of the program with some sense of their own, identity, values, and self-esteem."

T
he young people in the program "asked a lot of questions. Where did I grow up? Where did I go to school? Was I married? Do I have a dog? And I found that we were sort of becoming role models to these kids." Like the project's "hero walls," Jane Golden herself became "a sign of what they could be...symbolic of their potential in life"

Jane Golden grew up in Margate, California, drawing and painting from earliest childhood. She painted her first mural shortly after she graduated from Stanford University. Soon her vibrant murals were appearing everywhere. While painting a huge mural in Santa Monica, she grew ill. Told she was going to die, she moved to Philadelphia where she continues the fight against her disease atop a scaffold, committed to changing people's lives with her murals.

JANE GOLDEN

Golden says South Philadelphia, has changed since she arrived there. "If you could see what this looked like when I started working here.... The place was just filled with garbage and debris and these walls were peeling and covered with graffiti. But this is one of the privileges of my job, that I've come across some women who have just jumped in with both feet and have tackled the problems head on. I look at the women I work with in all the neighborhoods and I see how they keep fighting against the odds and I look at their accomplishments in the face of all the problems and I look at them as an inspiration and it helps keep me going."

Heroes 20 feet tall: you see them all over Philadelphia. At first the neighborhoods wanted nothing but waterfalls, landscapes. But Jane Golden asked people how they could get meaning in their walls. "There was an incredible amount of excitement," she says, "as they came up with the idea of putting themselves on the wall."

Now Philadelphians have many heroes to look up to—business leaders, Olympic heroes, sports stars like Julius Erving, historical figures, ethnic heroes, local heroes, the "real" heroes: men, women, and children loved and celebrated by their community.

Freedom and risk . . .

finding grounds for choices.

Rock climbers *Dan and Sue* McDevitt are scaling a peak in Yosemite National Park. A single bolt driven in the granite rock face is all that stands between them and the valley floor 3,000 feet below. They hang suspended above one of America's special places, a symbol as powerful as the Statue of Liberty, as precious as the freedom and beauty of wilderness itself. At the same time they are at the heart of a passionate debate over access to that wilderness.

Whose mountain is it anyway?

Climbing is a sport about the freedom to choose: every new route is a new enterprise. Each first ascent creates a new experience, a new possibility.

The McDevitts have been living and climbing in Yosemite for years. They have a home on the park's border and are guides for the Yosemite Mountaineering School. Sue says, "I feel lucky that we are able to do these climbs and hang out here on the rocks.

"We need to be responsible for the clients that we take up on these climbs. It's someone's life that we're bringing up here, so I'm sure they appreciate it when they see that nice big bolt instead of a 20-year-old bolt from way back when they first put them in." Dan adds, "Loose and old bolts are very common now because some of the bolts are over 35 or 40 years old, so they do loosen up and get rusty and actually fall out even if you just lean on them."

"In Yosemite we have four million visitors a year, and trying to maintain a near pristine wilderness with that many visitors is not an easy thing to do."

—MARK FINCHER, RANGER

For years rock climbing was an eccentric sport practiced by a small, close-knit community. In the past ten years the sport has burgeoned into one of the most popular outdoor recreational activities. New ascent routes have been bolted as quickly as climbers can re-sharpen their drill bits. Some 10,000 bolts have been drilled into Yosemite rock, according to Mark Fincher, a Yosemite ranger in charge of climbs in land designated as wilderness areas.

More climbers and more routes not only mean more bolts in the rock face, but new access trails, more trash, more automobiles, more disturbance of wild-life and vegetation. For the visionary climbers, bolts are the tools they need to be the Magellans of new climbs. But for some conservationists, bolts are tools of destruction, defacing the park.

Climber-environmentalists have claimed that pockmarking rock faces with fixed anchor bolts is so harmful "that entire cliffs are in danger of sheer-ing off, like icebergs calving from Alaskan glaciers," as Sam Davidson of *Rock and Ice* magazine ironically reported. The Wilderness Society wants existing bolts removed from all national parks and wilderness areas, and all bolts prohibited in the future. Authorities at the

"Everybody has their hobby or activity, and it just so happens that this is what we like to do."

Daniel Boone National Forest in Kentucky agreed and declared the setting of fixed bolts an act of "vandalism."

While some environmental groups admit that the bolt itself may not be a problem, the bolt is still the keystone to the issue: curtail bolting, they argue, perhaps by limiting the power drills that are used to set them, and other types of damage to these majestic mountains will also be reduced.

Climbers feel they are being unfairly targeted, that there are far more pressing environmental concerns in national parks: from traffic congestion to pollution and litter, from crime to destruction of vegetation—all a result of the "drive-by" tourists who visit national parks each year. They contrast the "paved paradise" of Yosemite Valley with the heights of Half Dome and El Capitan, whose many bolts are invisible from below.

But as more people visit the valley and more novices attempt rock climbs, issues of safety are a growing concern. Climbing accidents have increased in Yosemite. Many spectacular climbs would be impossible even for skilled traditional climbers if bolts were banned. Old bolts, new bolts, no bolts; which poses the greater risk—to the land and to the people?

"That's what wilderness designation is intended to do . . . to try to preserve those monuments—the heritage of our country."

—MARK FINCHER

Rangers, environmentalists, and climbers are trying to find common ground. After a workshop on "balancing recreational and resource protection needs" in national parks, Sam Davidson of *Rock and Ice* magazine spoke of the value of these discussions: "If climbing is to retain its basic character as an exercise in individual

"**W**ith the exception of a few spires and pinnacles, the South Dome is the only rock about the valley that is strictly inaccessible without artificial means, and its inaccessibility is expressed in severe terms. Nevertheless many a mountaineer, gazing admiringly, tried hard to invent a way to the top of its noble crown—all in vain until in the year 1875, George Anderson, an indomitable Scotchman, undertook the adventure…and resolutely drilled his way to the top, inserting eye-bolts five to six feet apart, and making his rope fast to each in succession, resting his feet on the last bolt while he drilled a hole for the next above….

"Climb the mountains and get their good tidings."

"On the 10th of November, after returning from a visit to Mount Shasta, a month or two after Anderson had gained the summit, I made haste to the Dome, not only for the pleasure of climbing, but to see what I might learn. The first winter storm-clouds had blossomed and the mountains and all the high points about the Valley were mantled in fresh snow. I was, therefore, a little apprehensive of danger from the slipperiness of the rope and the rock. Anderson himself tried to prevent me from making the attempt, refusing to believe that anyone could climb his rope in the snow-muffled condition in which it then was. Moreover, the sky was overcast and solemn snow-clouds began to curl around the summit, and my late experiences on icy Shasta came to mind. But reflecting that I had matches in my pocket, and that a little firewood might be found, I concluded that in case of a storm the night could be spent on the Dome without suffering anything worth minding, no matter what the clouds might bring forth. I therefore pushed on and gained the top."

—JOHN MUIR, *THE YOSEMITE*

imagination, skill, and judgment," he maintained, "a pragmatic resolution of this issue is essential."

But we must also strive to retain Yosemite's basic character. As Mark Fincher enthuses: "It's so great and awesome and it's still intact."

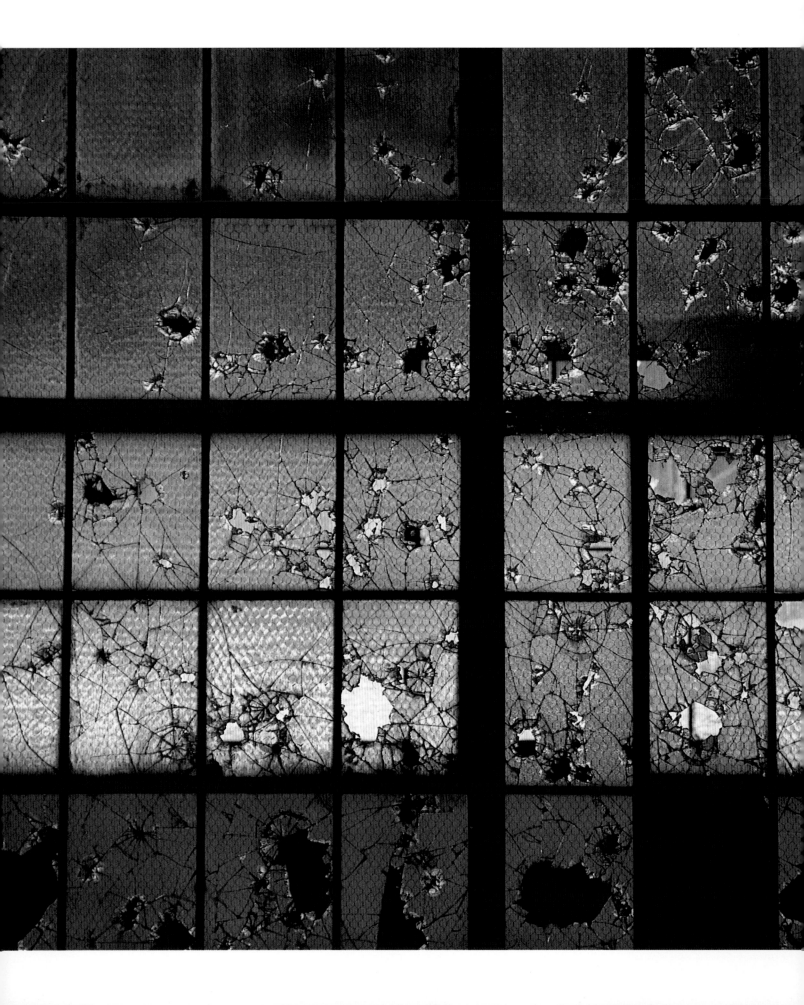

It's Up to Us!

When people fail to take responsibility, neglect spreads like an infection. When one window is broken, soon all of the surrounding windows will be broken. It is a sign that building owners and neighbors do not care.

Responsibility is empowerment;

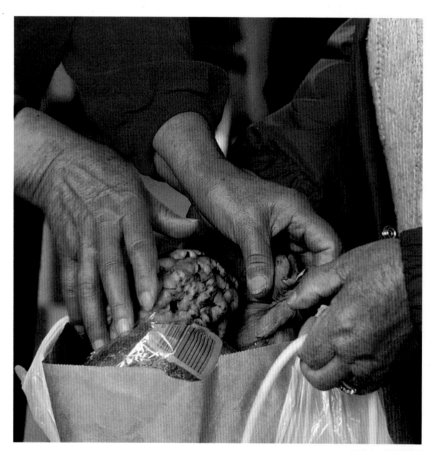

A S AMERICANS, MOST OF us have a strong idea of our rights, but a weak idea of our responsibilities. Professor Lawrence Friedman of Stanford University points out that Americans have recently come to claim all rights for themselves and assign all responsibilities to the government—forgetting that in a democracy we *are* the government. Rights make no sense without responsibilities: a responsibility to a shared community, for example, or to the common good, to our present, and to our children's future.

Responsibility is one of the unwritten guidelines that should determine our behavior. It is one of the necessary virtues, like "basic human decency, trust, and the willingness to get along" (in the words of former Maine commissioner Bill Brennan) that truly animate our society.

It is these unwritten responsibilities that must inform the actions of each citizen—the willingness to help our neighbors, serve on committees, care for our world. We must hold together our world, not expecting that others will take up the slack, not doing casual harm to one another by failing to do our share. Because when we fail, our community suffers.

Responsibility has too often been perceived as an unwelcome duty. Actually, it is a chance to grow. "Few things," said Booker T. Washington, "help an individual more than to place responsibility upon him and to let him know that you trust him." It is a gift of power: you cannot be responsible until you can act for and with others.

empowerment is in each person's hands.

> ❝**The worth of a state, in the long run, is the worth of the individuals composing it.**❞
>
> —JOHN STUART MILL

How goodness happens: It is a matter of individual conscience—and community values.

In what one historian called "a conspiracy of goodness," the 3,000 residents of Le Chambon-sur-Lignon, France, conspired to save the lives of 5,000 Jews during World War II. The villagers risked their own lives to save people they didn't know because it was the right thing to do.

Le Chambon is an old stone village, a small community in rural France, surrounded by farms, woods, and mountains. An old stone church is at the town center—a Huguenot church. Huguenot hymns boast that believers are strong as rock, steadfast in their resistance. Their Bible advises that one must "Seek good, and not evil, that ye may live."

"That ye may live." The citizens of Chambon—not only the Huguenots, but also Jews, and atheists—showed the value they put on human life by their deeds during four years of German occupation.

Chambonnais hid refugees against informers, moving them again and again to stay ahead of police, feeding them despite the common suffering from sickness, hunger, and cruelty, securing false identification papers, and guiding the refugees along escape routes.

While more than a million children were killed by the Nazis during the war, the tiny town of Le Chambon was the safest place for children on the continent of Europe.

Said one woman whose three children were sheltered by the people of Le Chambon, "The Holocaust was storm, lightning, thunder, wind, rain. And Le Chambon was the rainbow."

Community responsibility: personal empowerment and group power change the landscape of the poor in San Antonio.

San Antonio's Mexican-Americans had accepted flooding in their neighborhoods for years. The Hispanic *colonias* were built on low-lying ground. As San Antonio grew, new housing developments sent their runoff water spilling into the downstream colonias.

Wailed one woman whose home was lost, "Why is God punishing me like this?" Her neighbor replied, "It's not God, it's the developers."

By the early 1970s, roads closed with each heavy rain. Cars stalled. Schools could not open. An already powerless community was cut off from the rest of the world.

With each storm, homes would flood. Water rose through windows ruining possessions, ruining lives. Colonia residents were forced to raise their beds on rocks and bricks.

There were many sleepless nights, many tragedies as floodwaters swept through neighborhoods again and again. Families stood vigil watching for rising water. With every major storm, people—often children—were drowned.

Many of these poorest of the poor were raised to be afraid of activism. We had our dignity, they said, but we were humble, always polite.

So the community mood swung between fatalism and fury. Sometimes there was hot-headed talk about marching on city hall. More often there was a misplaced faith that city officials would get around to solving their problems sooner or later.

But it was the community itself, organizing to get on the city's agenda, taking reponsibility to create change, that rescued the poor of San Antonio from an endless cycle of misery.

"We just wait for the water to go down so we can take the dead dogs and garbage out of our neighborhoods, out of our yards."

Flooding was common in San Antonio's Hispanic districts, until residents discovered—and wielded—the power of community.

"Politics is the art of give and take."

"Power: from the root *posse,* 'to be able.' COPS makes power politics possible."

"People don't drown in our neighborhoods anymore." —George Ozuna

"Do you like standing in water?" Ernie Cortes asked Andres Sarabia after heavy rains flooded San Antonio's colonias.

"No."

"Then why are you?"

Ernie Cortes was a community organizer from Industrial Areas Foundation (IAF). His questions started community members on the way to taking control of their lives.

Getting people to think, to reflect, that's the first step, according to Andres Sarabia. "Why does it have to be this way?" Sarabia asked himself as he walked through streets that turned into open sewers with every storm.

It was his home. His neighborhood. His community. After he learned to act within that community, he became the first president of COPS, Communities Organized for Public Service.

The COPS organizing process turned people like Sarabia—people who had always been active in church and PTA activities—into community leaders who studied local problems and demanded solutions.

There was anger when COPS workers began to investigate city finances. They found that the money for drainage projects had been appropriated years before—but time after time it had been diverted to the wealthier neighborhoods of the city.

Cortes fanned the flames. "You are buying the gun that is going to kill you," he told Sarabia, referring to the bond money being diverted from his neighborhood. "Now what are you going to do about it?"

By 1975 Sarabia and COPS were confronting San Antonio's city council about the flooding in Mexican-American neighborhoods.

Explained Beatrice Gallego, another early COPS leader, "We wanted our fair share of city monies.

"But we had to go knocking and opening the doors. We had to pound really hard for them to hear us.

"There's no democracy unless you're working with it," Gallego states. "You're forcing democracy and you're forcing justice."

ANDRES SARABIA
According to Sarabia:

"The mayor asked the city manager how long the city had known of the flooding problem.

"City manager replied, 'Forty years.'

"'Well, how many people does it affect?'

"City manager answered, 'A hundred thousand.'

"The mayor asked, 'Why hasn't anyone done anything?'

"City manager said, 'No one ever complained.'

"We've been complaining ever since!"

When community organizer Ernie Cortes first asked Beatrice Gallego about problems in her neighborhood, she laughed at him.

"What's not a problem?" she replied.

"We have no drains, no sidewalks, no curbs, no parks, we're cut in half by an expressway, we don't have enough water pressure to water our yards and draw bathwater at the same time."

Public power and what Hannah Arendt calls

COPS is about "stepping up to the microphone, it's speaking, it's listening; and then it's being willing to act collaboratively with other people."

The story of COPS according to *Cold Anger* by Mary Beth Rogers, is "a story about a new kind of intervention in politics by working poor people who incorporate their religious values into a struggle for power and visibility. It is about women and men…who promote public and private hope, political and personal responsibility, community and individual transformation. Even joy."

Where is that joy found?

"The church, the family, and the schools," says Ed Chambers of the IAF Training Institute. Where else would you find the power of the poor? Chambers taught Cortes that "the greatest potential resides in the institutions that people are loyal to and pay their money to and are willing to sacrifice for."

The power of COPS grows from human values. COPS attracts people whose values are "based on the belief in the fundamental worth of the individual," according to Rogers, and the belief that "only within the framework of a caring human 'community' could the individual grow, develop, and rise to his or her potential.

"To Cortes and the people he was bringing to the political process, a 'citizen' is someone who matters, someone who becomes visible—and thus worthy —by taking action to benefit the common good."

A concept of justice is essential to defining the common good. COPS has shown that political power can help to ensure that justice is carried out. As Thucydides said, "The standard of justice depends on the equality of power."

To build intellectual capital, Ernie Cortes has his students read the Greeks. But Sister Christine Stephens, member of a San Antonio-based teaching order and IAF leader, sees a biblical vision of justice in his work:

"I was always very nervous talking in public, but Ernie sat me down one night and talked about what it meant

"the joy of public happiness"

COPS has a membership of 27 dues-paying Catholic churches in San Antonio. It works with Metro Alliance, which has a membership of 23 Protestant and Catholic churches, to unite 90,000 of the poorest families in San Antonio for political power.

Movements that have started with these organizations include QUEST, a job training program that located a source of high-paying jobs in health care, secured promises of jobs and then trained people to fill them.

Women—some "real powerhouses" according to Cortes—have taken strong leadership roles in COPS. Over the years, several women have been president of COPS, a "reward for results."

COPS leader Beatrice Gallego says, "We really had to fight for that respect" in city hall. "We really had to make them understand that we want to be part of the decision-making process."

> ❝Organizing is a fancy word for relationship building.❞
> —SAYS IAF ORGANIZER CORTES.
> COPS ORGANIZATION, HE SAYS, IS
> ABOUT "GIVING PEOPLE A PUBLIC LIFE."

"Power is such a good thing, everyone should have some."
—ERNIE CORTES

Making her move.

to be a public person. How your true self is just over your shoulder where you can't see it, and how the only way you can know yourself is to see it reflected in someone else."

For 20 years COPS workers have seen their true selves reflected in their good works and in their community. As they grow into responsibility and a new sense of power.

This is the lesson taught by Frances Moore Lappé and Paul Martin Du Bois in "Power in a Living Democracy": that most people understand power as bullying: unilateral, manipulative, corrupt, dirty. Which leads to the conviction that "powerlessness must be virtuous." But, according to Cortes, "powerlessness corrupts too." Relational power and reciprocity—the transformative power of two people working together—is accountable, accessible, and full of potential.

"In our work for social justice," say Lappé and Du Bois, "it is tempting to view some sources of power as relatively fixed, beyond change. Sometimes the power of wealth or institutionalized positions appear unmovable. But they are only the most visible sources of power. Other sources, harder to see, are more fluid: information and knowledge,

image, persuasiveness based on truth and reason, and the impact of numbers—numbers of people and the quality of their commitment, their willingness to persevere.

"The challenge of living democracy is consciously emphasizing relationships that develop these fluid, dynamic sources of power. And this is precisely the genius of the most successful community-based citizen organizing."

ERNIE CORTES

COPS recently celebrated its 20th anniversary. Its greatest—and probably most lasting—achievement has been in growing leadership and power within the community. "We've tried," says Cortes, "to teach this whole Jeffersonian notion of 'renewal and reorganization,' constantly trying to bring new people, leaders, into the organization.

"You can't have the same leadership in the center of the organization for 20 or 25 years." COPS' new leaders may well move through San Antonio's new community center.

Before COPS changed the face of San Antonio, teens would swim in the filthy lakes that formed in the streets whenever their neighborhoods flooded. Now their parents' dedication has brought the community a new swimming pool as well as a host of educational programs.

Edmund Burke said, "The only thing necessary for evil to prevail is for good men to do nothing."

Ernie Cortes won't let them. That's what IAF grassroots organizing is all about—training in responsibility, engagement, public action. Cortes says:

"If I had to define in one sentence what organizing is all about, it's identifying and testing out and developing leadership. The whole notion of leadership—it's like education. Think about it: the word is from the Latin *e-ducere*, which means literally to draw out, to lead out. So there's always been that leadership dimension in the whole notion of education.

"And that's what the central focus of the organization is: that development of leadership through action —action around issues that are connected to family and property and education. Which is what Aristotle said politics is all about—discussion, conversations, public debate, public discourse about family, property, and education. That's what we're trying to teach in developing these organizations, how to do politics or how to have these conversations.

"But if the politics is going to be meaningful, there has to be a dimension of transformation that takes place—and that's only going to occur to the extent that people begin to understand what we mean by this kind of power called relational power. Which is not only acting on but allowing other people to act on you....

"You begin to share your interest, your story, with other people and allow them to act on you, to challenge you, and then begin to reweave your story. So it becomes connected to other people's stories...in public political conversations.

"But these conversations have to lead to action, they have to lead to public engagement, public drama—where there's real negotiation about issues that matter."

Responsibility. Traditional value. A tribal remembrance to guide the Inupiat future.

The Inupiat, who live in northwest Alaska, have one foot in the modern, one in the ancient world. Their towns have been invaded by stateside immigrants, by TV sitcoms and junk food, but they still survive mainly by hunting whale, caribou, bear, and seal.

When they go hunting among the shifting blocks of ice in Kotzebue Sound, they may carry Walkmans, but they do not carry compasses. They carry maps in their minds—detailed memories of local landscapes—that allow them to move swiftly and surely through their dazzling world.

Now their tribal memories are creating a compass for their community as they look to traditional values of responsibility and respect to guide them into the future.

"Our forefathers were contained here and they were preoccupied with gathering food and survival. And now we're forced to think in terms of formal education and upward mobility and commerce with other people. And that's happened in a very short time."

—Elder Rachel Craig

Twelve years ago, the tiny Inupiat town of Kotzebue, 26 miles above the Arctic Circle, was blighted by violence, drug and alcohol abuse, and a sense of despair. Self-determination has changed their lives.

After 7,000 Inupiat in northwest Alaska moved to incorporate their own government in 1980, Kotzebue's elders and a regional social service agency formed Inupiat Ilitqusiat to guide government policy.

Inupiat Ilitqusiat translates as traditional values, and the program of community responsibility that began with a statement of those values has had a marked effect on the villagers. Significant drops in crime and also in suicides are attributed to this renewed emphasis on traditional ways—and to new restrictions on alcohol in the community.

Special youth camps, school and radio programs, court and business policies set up by tribal elders all reinforce traditional values.

"Through our extended family we retain, teach, and live our Inupiat way."

Teaching traditional values has a very real meaning to Inupiat society. Traditions may well mean survival.

Hunting, fishing, and food gathering put food on Inupiat tables. Each year brings a round of hunting. Caribou are a staple of the traditional Inupiat diet—that's why Inupiat businesses offer time off to employees so they can track migrating caribou in season.

In spring Inupiat people move to seal-hunting camps on the ice along the coast near Sisaulik. Elders show youngsters how to set up a traditional camp and teach them how to hunt seal—not only the techniques of the hunt, but also the rituals that bind their community.

Elders also run Spirit Camps in the summer. This is "hands-on" training for young children. The elders teach fishing skills, such as how to make and set a net. How to cut fish and dry it. Practical training includes lessons in dogsledding, firewood gathering, and berry picking. Students learn to live with children from other villages. Spiritual training imparts the values of the culture.

The old ways must not be forgotten. Community esteem—"the respect and admiration that you give to the person for living their life for the good of the community—is something you cannot buy," an elder says. "It must be given to you."

When the work is all done, there is still time for community fun.

"To walk in two worlds with one spirit," that is the Inupiat way.

The Inupiats' "two worlds" according to Rachel Craig:

"The kind of society our forefathers built on cooperation, on sharing, on looking after the fatherless, the widows, the old people . . . that on top of becoming literate in the white man's world, learning about his culture, about his religion, that should have made the quality of our life better."

"We are all united when we make a commitment to teach values to our children," says Bertha Jennings, former Coordinator of Inupiat Ilitqusiat. Today Kotzebue has its own schools. When Jennings was growing up she had no choice but to go to a Bureau of Indian Affairs boarding school more than 1,000 miles from her home.

Inupiat carry their tribal compass in their pockets. Traditional values —selected after spirited debate in village meetings—have been printed on wallet-sized cards issued to each member of the Inupiaq community. Their statement of beliefs starts and ends with responsibility:

Every Inupiaq is responsible to all other Inupiat for the survival of our cultural spirit, and the values and traditions through which it survives. Through our extended family, we retain, teach, and live our Inupiaq way. With guidance and support from our elders, we must teach our children Inupiaq values:

Knowledge of Language	**Sharing**
Respect for Others	**Cooperation**
Respect for Elders	**Love for Children**
Knowledge of Family Tree	**Hard Work**
Avoid Conflict	**Respect for Nature**
Spirituality	**Humor**
Family Roles	**Hunter Success**
Domestic Skills	**Humility**
Responsibility to Tribe	

The words are also written on posters throughout the community and repeated often by everyone from village elders to radio DJ's to local judges.

Against forgetting.

"An elder's voice...that's my dictionary," says Jeanie Greene, producer of *Heartbeat Alaska* of Rural Alaska Television Network. "If an elder tells me something, that's good enough for me."

An elder's voice might save the young people of the community. "Why our young people began to kill themselves," said Rachel Craig, "is something we haven't really understood. I don't know why there's so much despair. It's so opposite from what the elders tell us, 'I hope you'll live a long life.' To them life was a gift. When we start teaching the Inupiat Ilitqusiat to our children at a young age, they have the satisfaction within themselves...that life is good."

The young listen as elders pass down their memories. Elders collect and record tribal stories, which provide a thread of continuity for their culture. Wisdom and humor, and the constant theme of survival mark many of these songs and tales.

Here is an Inuit song as remembered by Peter Matthiessen in "Annals of Conservation: Survival of the Hunter." He was visiting a hunting camp: "At the campfire, Navarana sang a song about some unfortunate little auks that had to fly south without their young, because jaegers and gulls had taken all the eggs. But the Inuhuit are nothing if not pragmatic in their harsh and unrelenting struggle for survival, and so she added, 'We children cried and cried for those little auks, because we were afraid we would not get any to eat.'"

As traditional culture meets modern technology—radio and TV transmit the elders' tales, hunting starts to give way to grocery shopping, snowmobiles replace dogsleds as motorboats have forced out kayaks—the Inupiat are determined not to let the wave of the future wash away memories of the past.

Language, values, self-esteem—the Inupiat cultural heritage.

The Inupiat are spreading the word about their heritage. Inupiat stories and cultural programs air on public radio each day, with 25% of them broadcast in the Inupiat language.

And Inupiat elders have traveled from their home to visit indigenous people in Russia, Canada, and Greenland to discuss the problems they share. Almost every native group in Alaska has followed the Inupiat lead to reaffirm traditional values.

"In traditional hunting, land and life belong to every member of a community . . . mute sea ice and empty land . . . are the ground of a hard life, providing a sense of continuity and tradition which lies at the heart of Inuhuit well-being. Hunting is the vital nerve of Inuhuit existence."

—PETER MATTHIESSEN

"Education was introduced to us. The political system was introduced to us. Everything that came from outside was introduced to us and we had to learn it. They never said, 'Well, be yourself.'"

—RACHEL CRAIG

The seal hunt is an important tradition for the Inupiat. The first seal to be killed is returned to the village, where the successful hunter gives the meat to others, the young and old of the village. Sharing, learning to give, as well as to take.

The Inupiat say, "When we share what we have, the food that we have, it makes our spirits feel good."

Sharing the spirit. Life is a gift. Food is a gift.

Democracy is like exercise. A little leads to more.

In an innovative school program, high school students in Fort Myers, Florida, learn democracy first-hand by taking personal responsibility for their environment.

The Monday Group, an environmental studies class, takes on an annual project in the community. On the class curriculum: "helping students acquire and refine skills through practical experience in addressing significant community problems."

Knowledge is power. The students' message has been heard.

Fifteen years ago, the Monday Group saved the Six-Mile Cypress Swamp from development. This 2,500-acre cypress stand on the edge of Fort Myers was acquired when the students initiated and helped pass a county referendum funding the purchase.

Then students used their knowledge of botany and biology to provide technical assistance to the County Parks and Recreation Department. They helped develop a master plan for the area, which is now a park that is often used as an outdoor classroom.

Each year teacher Rick Tully leads new students into the swamp's cypress stand. "Look what kids like you have done! Think about it. What do you kids want to do?"

Diversity, change, interdependence —the same rules apply in school and in the natural world.

"Responsibility is the first step in responsibility." —W.E.B. Du Bois

"Every time a student comes back from a meeting with the county commissioner," says teacher Rick Tully, "I've got a new insight as to how things are working."

Since 1969, groups of Lee County high school students—and their teacher—have been meeting all day every other Monday to learn not just about ecology but also participatory democracy. Students spend the first quarter of the school year researching local environmental issues. The students vote to select a project to work on as a group. The project is an exercise in teamwork, democracy in the classroom.

The project must involve student lobbying of the county commission, the most powerful local political body. In this way, students become masters of local politics. They learn how to communicate complicated and controversial ideas to the media, to politicians, and to their classmates. They learn not only natural sciences but also the key arts of political action.

The group has created a manatee education site, preserved beach and swamp areas, launched recycling and ethanol production projects. Graduates of the group may not plan on having political careers, but, they say, "they will be involved."

The lone cowboy. An American myth.
A response to the Western landscape.
In Jane Hollister Wheelwright's words,
"the fantastic beauty, the rugged-
ness, the physical uniqueness
and the cruelty of the ranch
lands" of America have shaped
our sense of self and
of community.

It Takes All of Us

T HE LONER, THE OUTSIDER, the rebel—our society has a strange fascination with this figure. A love/hate relationship. So many times the heroes in our society seem to work in isolation. How wonderful when our families and our communities reveal to us a different kind of hero. These ordinary people, these everyday heroes go about the necessary tasks of caring for young and old, of helping and healing, of rekindling our collective spirit.

In honoring these everyday heroes we celebrate the traditional joy of involvement in a group, the special energy from participation. Some of these heroes are teachers, mentors; they all are role models. Showing us a way to work within the community, they teach us to find our voice, to find our place.

These not always glamorous but always inspiring people live in a way that demonstrates the finest human capacities, the highest ideals. As they work to create a better world, a more perfect society, they show us the value of long-term commitments to people and places, the value of dreams, the value of a hard-eyed appreciation of reality.

The first lesson of participation: instead of hanging back—an outsider looking in, cynical, disaffected, suspicious, a victim bemoaning a harsh and hopeless fate—instead of retreating from problems, take that first step to join a group. A school group, church group, social group, community group, group of friends, group of neighbors. There truly is strength in numbers. The more you do together, the more you *can* do.

Lt. James (Rocky) Robinson is a paramedic, a New York City emergency medical service supervisor. Has been for 25 years. There is one thing that really used to get to him, he says.

"I used to see all of these volunteer ambulance services in other communities, and what was happening, it was an entrance way into the NYC Emergency Medical Service. It's the entrance way for doctors, nurses, firemen, policemen. They use it as a springboard for success. But something used to boggle my mind. I never saw a volunteer corps in Harlem or in Williamsburg, Brooklyn. So I felt like the reason why we didn't have as many minority medical professionals was because we didn't have the entrance way for these people. You had to have some type of influence. You had to have some kind of money to get into the system. So I felt that we had to do something ourself in our own community in order to be role models for our kids, in order to get jobs for the people in the community.

"And the response time in poor neighborhoods—the time it took for an ambulance to answer a call—was three times more than in the affluent neighborhoods. One of the reasons for that was the volunteerism in those communities. I got the idea from Art Zolar to start the same type of service in Bed-Stuy that they had in the Jewish communities. They really were my inspiration.

"So what happened is me and my partner decided to start a volunteer ambulance in Bed-Stuy. But when we first started, people were laughing us right off the street. They said, 'What the hell you talking about? We're not going to subsidize a volunteer ambulance corps in a community where they already have a 911 system.'"

People stopped laughing when they saw that the volunteers were there to "supplement" city service. Call after call, time after time, the corps provided rapid response—they saved lives. And gave hope to the community's teens.

When news of the service got out, Rocky says, there was a lot less "stereotyping of Bed-Stuy. We got letters from all over the nation, saying, 'We're proud of you.'"

Emergency services rescue a community. The

"**This service is about how you feel about your neighbor. People were dying in the street and we did something about it. We're about saving lives and changing lives.**" —AMBULANCE VOLUNTEER

Violence is no stranger on the streets of Bedford-Stuyvesant in New York. Knives, guns, drugs; dealers, gang-bangers; boarded up buildings and abandoned souls.

Call 911 and you could bleed to death waiting for a city ambulance to arrive.

Lt. James (Rocky) Robinson, a city paramedic, and his friend Joe Perez knew that they could do better. Together they set up a volunteer ambulance service.

Now, according to Robinson, the Bedford-Stuyvesant Volunteer Ambulance Corps has become "the catalyst for a healing process that is happening in our neighborhood."

Bedford-Stuyvesant Volunteer Ambulance Corps. . .

"People call us because they trust us. Our only politics are to get things done. We cruise the neighborhood, help the homeless. . . . And we deliver lots of babies. That's the best feeling, the best high in the world."

—RUDY BOYD, CHIEF OF STAFF

...shows residents "how to care about

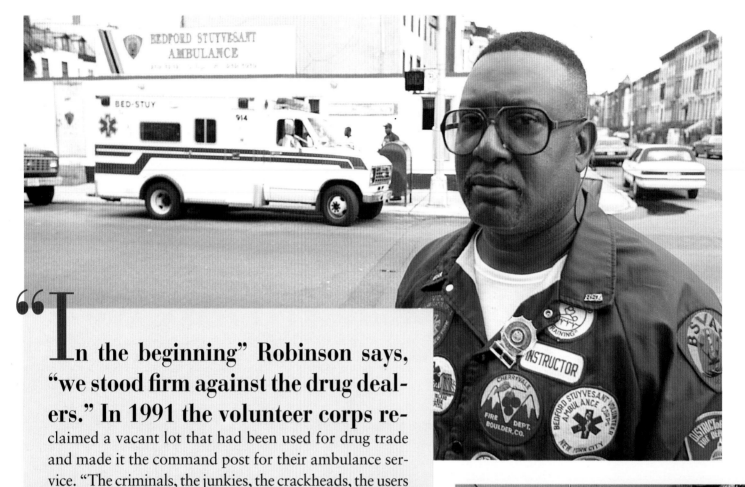

"**I**n the beginning" Robinson says, "we stood firm against the drug dealers." In 1991 the volunteer corps reclaimed a vacant lot that had been used for drug trade and made it the command post for their ambulance service. "The criminals, the junkies, the crackheads, the users said they were going to burn our trailer, if we didn't get our trailer off that corner," says Rocky. "But we would not listen."

Today a 50-foot trailer sits on that lot, a visible symbol of community perseverance, the will to survive. The service has taken a lot of the neighborhood kids' fascination with danger and channeled it toward positive results. Through a group called the Trauma Troopers, kids 6 to 21 learn to be "life savers, not life takers."

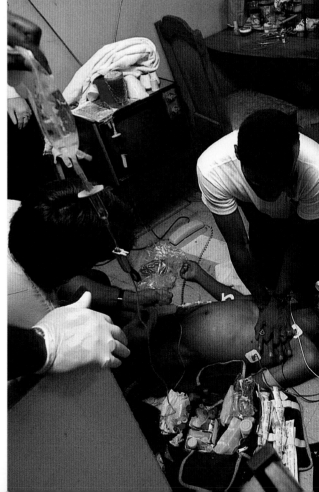

"I've turned my living room over to the Corps for classroom space, because those classes got me off welfare. I took the course and didn't know how to drive; they taught me how on a used ambulance. Now I have a job with the city EMS and I'm teaching others. —Deborah Crawford, Commander and Driver

themselves, their neighbors and the community."

The Trauma Troopers describes itself as "80 gang members...a boys and girls challenging club." The TT program can teach kids "to be the good guy instead of the villain. The Program "can change the scenario from funerals to graduations." The Program offers an "alternative to the life of drugs, crime, and violence that most of them take for granted."

"Some things they teach you can't be found in books," explained Tonya Olmo, a young volunteer dispatcher whose move to the Corps obviously taught her a lot. " People here talk to you and care about you."

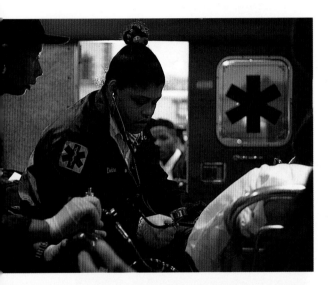

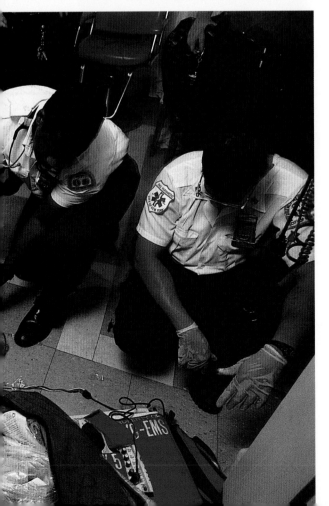

LOG BOOK SATURDAY

9:00 P.M. Car crash at Tompkins and Macon. Two parties injured, one with difficulty breathing.

9:31 P.M. Male shot. DOA.

9:55 P.M. Teen stabbed at Marcus Garvey and Monroe. Blood loss.

10:25 P.M. Two-year-old girl with difficulty breathing. Heart defect.

10:45 P.M. Man having seizures. Probable drug reaction.

11:00 P.M. Six-year-old boy struck by hit-and-run driver.

11:12 P.M. Bicyclist sideswiped by car.

11:16 P.M. Fight in progress at housing project.

11:26 P.M. Drunken incoherent woman.

11:55 P.M. Male shot. The second life saved tonight. Cause for celebration in a neighborhood where there's often not much to smile about.
—ROBERT FLEMING,
RESCUING A NEIGHBORHOOD:
THE BEDFORD-STUYVESANT
VOLUNTEER AMBULANCE CORPS

"Chief Boyd likes taking young people out on the calls, to let them experience at a young age what real life is like. If I wasn't here I'd have messed my life up by now"—YOUNG VOLUNTEER

Long hours, tough decisions, tense situations—all are part of emergency care. New York City is the toughest in the nation, handling more than a million calls yearly. And 75% of emergency medical calls in New York City come from minority neighborhoods, many of them coping with rampant crime and staggering poverty. City or hospital ambulance crews, says Robinson, "sometimes forget that they're dealing with human beings. If you don't have any compassion, then you should not be doing this." And the corps finds people to do the work—it has trained more than 500 volunteers. Says Robinson, "These people really are the heroes, because they're the ones that have saved the lives."

"Real heroes don't wear gold chains, they wear lifesaving medals."

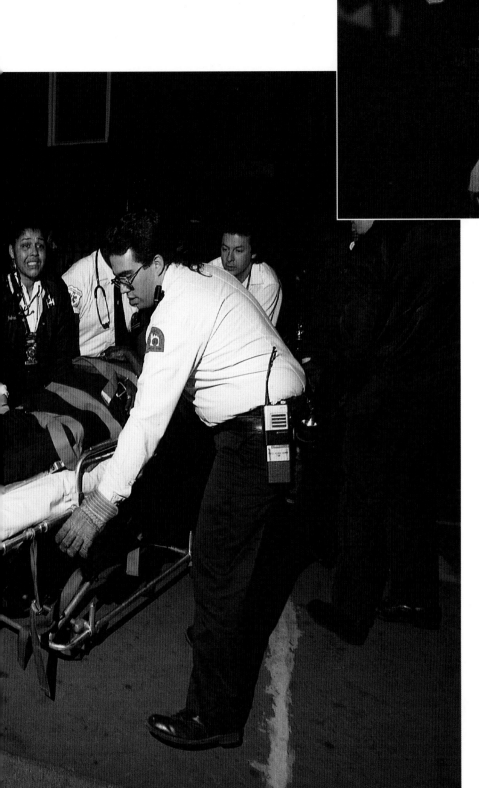

The Bedford-Stuyvesant Volunteer Ambulance Corps (BSVAC) currently runs two to three ambulances anywhere from 16 to 24 hours a day.

BSVAC also teaches first aid and CPR to the teens in the community. The program has made careers as EMTs or physician's assistants real possibilities for neighborhood residents. LaGuardia, a nearby college, sends students to BSVAC for training. Private ambulance companies call BSVAC when they have a position to fill: they know the volunteers have hours of experience and extensive training.

But the corps teaches more. It teaches young people to respect life. BSVAC imparts "the art of saving lives. Not just the physical and practical aspects, but also the emotional side. The mind-set," says Rocky, "is the most important thing."

"With CPR, you don't have to be a mental giant. All you got to do is care about somebody. If you care, you can make a difference." —ROCKY ROBINSON

Participation can be a good lesson in

> **"Good things come to he who waits. But he who works, well, he does a lot better."**
>
> —CHUCK KAPARICH

When Chuck Kaparich sees a carousel his eyes light up. "Carousels! They're just so pretty! How could you not want to go galloping away on a horse? How could you not fall in love with them when you see 40 horses standing there, every one of them different, every one of them saying, 'Ride me.' You just can't imagine not wanting to do that."

His enthusiasm was infectious. People in his hometown of Missoula, Montana, could not imagine not wanting to help him bring his dream to life. They volunteered to work thousands of hours, carving, painting, building a carousel for their town, no matter that "the only pay you get is the joy of the work."

Chuck says of the hundreds of "big-hearted" people who shared his dream, "This is a family."

And the whole family turned out to celebrate the opening of the carousel.

the art of the possible—

Pictured at top, from left: Greg Dalton, Pam Copley, Greg Bennett, Phil Hall. Above: Theresa and Randy Cox.

The completed carousel measures more than 40 feet across and has 38 horses in three circles, as well as two wheelchair accessible chariots. It revolves to the tunes of a 400-pipe band organ that duplicates the sounds of 23 instruments and 45 musicians—playing mainly marches and foxtrots, the classic music of the carousel.

"Ride and smile," said Randy J. Cox, president of A Carousel for Missoula Foundation, "because the carousel belongs to you." It is "beauty and life and laughter, blended in a unique package."

Page D1

50 CENTS

alt

nty Attorney
urt
en looked at
Texas."
ventually left
ned to
e stolen
ities said.
stice of the
day afternoon
recognizance.

CAROUSEL
It opens today
with parade
and fireworks

Chuck Kaparich's dream to build a carousel for Missoula becomes reality today.
At noon, with help from the

A Carousel FOR Missoula

"The need to collectively build something that is beautiful and lasting." It is a deeply felt human need. The people of Missoula, Montana, felt that need.

"I see it as a gift the city is giving to itself," said Chuck Kaparich of the only "truly community-made carousel" in America. It took "a little magic dust" to bring the project to completion.

According to Kaparich, "I went to the city and I said 'Here's the deal. I'll make you the first hand-carved carousel in America in 60 years if you'll give me a piece of land in the riverside park.' That spot just sort of fit the dream.

"And there happened to be a newsman at that meeting and he ran a little article in the newspaper and I was besieged by letters and donations. And that was the first time I was aware that anyone else gave a damn.

"I had the first four ponies I carved myself. And I decided to hold a carving class to find people to help me carve the ponies. The class filled up in ten minutes with a waiting list of 100 people."

It took three years and involved hundreds of volunteers—the youngest 11, the oldest over 80—to build the carousel and move it to its home in the park: many designers, as well as 45 carvers, 6 sanders, 11 painters, a beau-

especially when participation

tician for the ponies' real horsehair tails, 15 glassworkers for the stained glass, 15 mechanics and engineers, plus framers to put up the grand central pole of the new carousel building.

A Carousel for Missoula Foundation was formed to take care of administrative matters. It did grass-roots fundraising—there were carousel T-shirts, carousel posters and calendars—and established an adoption fund by which individuals and groups could sponsor a horse. More than 40 groups and individuals paid for wood and paint and jewels for horses, naming them Sweet Sue, Red Ribbon, Big Sky Gaiety. Schoolkids who wanted to share in the project donated three tons of "Pennies for Ponies."

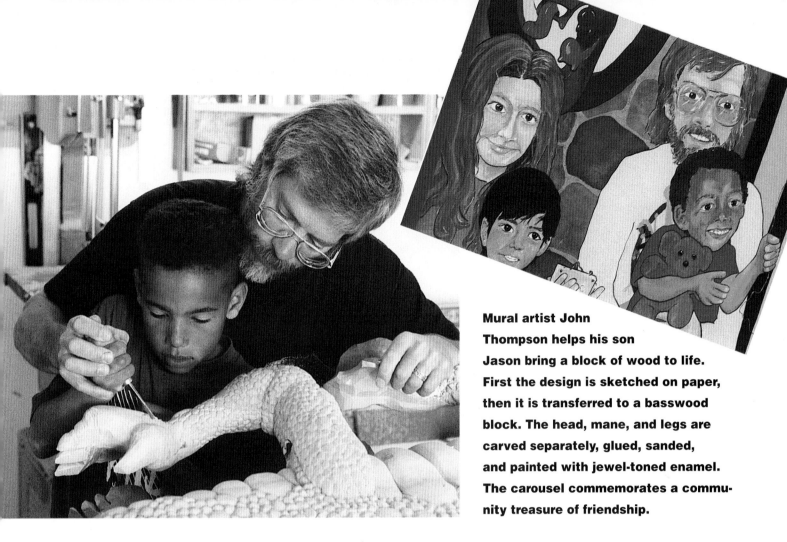

Mural artist John Thompson helps his son Jason bring a block of wood to life. First the design is sketched on paper, then it is transferred to a basswood block. The head, mane, and legs are carved separately, glued, sanded, and painted with jewel-toned enamel. The carousel commemorates a community treasure of friendship.

makes a community's dream come true.

How Chuck Kaparich came to love carousels: "As a kid growing up in a mining town that was poor and dirty, there was just this jewel up on the side of the mountain—Columbia Gardens carousel." He would ride and ride, listen to the band organ and watch the horses. No other carousel, he says, will ever "match the one I remember in my head."

Kaparich thought, "If they could do this a hundred years ago why couldn't someone do it today?" The same sense of history inspired many of the workers on the project.

Volunteer artists were "sensitive to the past by replicating an authentic carousel" and also "true to the present by mirroring the character of the northwest in their work."

Missoulians felt that "in this age of rapid change, it is important to cling to and preserve what is of positive value to our society. Because of its community-building potential and benefits to children, the carousel is an American institution that should be preserved." (Proposal for *Building an Artistic, Hand-Carved Wooden Carousel: A Remembrance of America's Cultural Past*)

At organ, left: Don Stinson, Scott Olson.

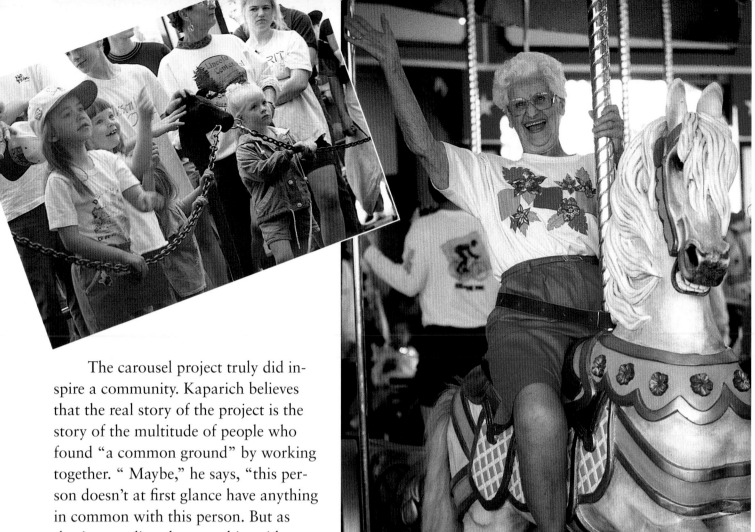

The carousel project truly did inspire a community. Kaparich believes that the real story of the project is the story of the multitude of people who found "a common ground" by working together. " Maybe," he says, "this person doesn't at first glance have anything in common with this person. But as they're standing there working side by side, you can't deny they do."

"In the true sense of the word, it is a community because we have a common goal and we work toward that goal, and we care about each other.

"It's the best of the community, the wonderful part I get to work with every day."

"Everybody is a kid today!" a volunteer cried, as the carousel cranked into action on May 27, 1995, a day Missoulians will not soon forget.

"Sometimes, we just need to have fun."

"I think in everyone's head there's a story that's equal to or exceeds my own, in terms of why they do this, why they love this, and why they care about this project," says Kaparich. "And for some people it's their children and their grandchildren; and for some people it's the artistry of the wood; and for some people it's just the camaraderie of the group. But everyone has their own story."

"The people here are individual thinkers. They're free spirited. They bicker. They fight. They argue. They vary from the left to the right.

"But when you get them all pointed in one direction, there is so much energy there. You know, some wonderful things can happen when everyone pushes in one direction.

"It's an intriguing equation, the community—and all the potential in a community that so seldom gets realized."

—CHUCK KAPARICH

Dan Kemmis, mayor of Missoula, wrote to A Carousel for Missoula Foundation: "Few communities will ever

experience a project so full of vitality, goodwill, public support. You and all the hundreds of volunteers who are making this dream come true through your selfless efforts have earned the gratitude of Missoulians for generations to come."

Kemmis, too, has initiated some projects that enhance civic life in Missoula. To stress community commitment to a shared way of life, he founded the Mayor's Roundtable, which opens city policy discussions to a group of ordinary citizens.

Kemmis also meets the public at the Missoula Farmer's Market. The market is a classic civic space; there are always lots of things going on there—chatting, eating, drinking, buying, selling—social, political, cultural, economic transactions.

Kemmis is eloquent about the role of such an event and space in the life of a community.

"I love watching the connections among people that get built here," he says. "It's so rich and accessible. It crosses generations. People bring their parents here when they come to town. People bring their babies as soon as they're born. It's almost sacramental—a kind of baptism where the community greets the child. There is an incredible web of relationships here which is so sustaining to people."

Kemmis, author of *Community and the Politics of Place,* acts on his belief that politics takes practice and a commitment to place. When Kemmis "holds court" at the Farmer's Market, "It makes things happen in a way they wouldn't otherwise."

DAN KEMMIS

"Getting them all pointed in one direction." That is Chuck Kaparich's description of how people get together to pursue a goal.

For Dan Kemmis, community action and communication depend on a sense of the interrelationships of a community, how "people's fates are woven together," The good life that each person wants depends on others "being secured in a different but equally good life."

Two ways to think about individual and group goals, about the common good.

"This ain't work," says Gene Hanks of Ely, Nevada, about a cattle round-up. "Work is when you do stuff you don't like." What he calls "a gather" is a real community event. Maybe 30 adults, and children besides.

"All been riding horses since they were tiny," Hank says. "They're out in the high desert country at seven A.M. Then there's a cookout for all the people that helped out.

"A lot of good people among ranchers," he says. "You bet."

"*…Each*

PART TWO

singing

By THE PEOPLE

what

HARD CHOICES

belongs

INFORMATION

to him

DELIBERATION

or her…"

"Democracy is always a beckoning goal, not a safe harbor. For freedom is an unremitting endeavor, never a final achievement."

—FELIX FRANKFURTER

DEMOCRACY IS THE CLAY to be shaped by each generation. How will today's Americans shape democracy, how can we work together to create today's democratic society? How will we make the hard choices that we face? There are strategies and tools to use in making difficult decisions. We must become informed and get involved in the process of deliberation. We must learn to evaluate information and to

employ it effectively in making our decisions, and we must learn to act on our beliefs and exercise our right to choose the best course.

Values, knowledge, judgment: these are the practical tools for evaluating information and making the decisions that we face as we work together to keep the American promise.

It is not enough to know the basic tenets of democracy, to understand the problems we face, to discuss the central questions of democratic life. It is not enough to defend the right of free speech. It is not enough to talk about the issues that we face as citizens. The next step is to learn how to work together to make the hard choices, to learn how to reach compromises, decisions that further the common good.

Our society provides us with the opportunity to examine a wide range of viewpoints; we must learn to sift through that glut of information. Be open to new ideas and alternatives. Practice tolerance for contrasting and opposing views.

Knowledge and the power to make hard choices. These are the tools of democratic life, the keys to a society "of the people, by the people, and for the people." Each of us must make the essential individual choices that will help preserve our collective freedoms, that will allow us each to rejoice—as did Wendell Berry in "The Wild Rose"—that "once more I am blessed, choosing again what I chose before."

For many people, voting is the key to the democratic process. Although democracy demands much more than that of its citizens, our responsibilities as voters in a representative system of government do involve some essential tools and skills. In this respect, 14th-century Florence, while not a democracy, can help to shed light on the theory and practice of citizen rule.

In the Florentine republic, leading citizens and members of 21 guilds had no choice but to participate in electoral politics. Potential officeholders were scrutinized by a committee of 144 members; a two-thirds majority of this group selected candidates for public office. The names of approved candidates were written on slips of paper and put in a bag. The bag, in turn, was placed in a locked chest, then placed inside another locked chest.

At election time, three processionals met in the grand hall of the Palazzo Vecchio. The locked chest was brought forward. A pair of monks (from different orders, to prevent conspiracy) each presented a key. The keys were taken by officials with great ceremony. The chests were unlocked, one after another; the bag was drawn from the inner chest. The officials drew out slips of paper at random, and they called out names. This was the selection of officeholders.

This ceremony was repeated every two months, since terms of office were only two months long. Every other month there were processions and "elections," with officeholders coming and going in a steady stream.

The consequences of this system were interesting. Leading citizens had to stay informed and had to pay careful attention to governmental affairs since they might be pressed into service at any time. They tended to be less critical of officeholders than today's voters because they knew they might be officeholders in their turn.

Hard choices represent society's balancing act. Is it possible to walk the line between extreme positions? One thing for sure, staying on the fence is not the way to keep society on the straight and narrow. Finding common ground is a means of survival.

HARD CHOICES

Who Said It Would Be Easy?

WHEN PUSH COMES TO SHOVE. When we have to make hard choices. We encounter these choices on an individual level when we confront our knowledge of freedom and limits.

When people are at odds. We encounter the same dilemmas on a social level when a community must make a decision that has no easy or clearcut answer or when all sides of an argument are compelling and when the pressures within a community come close to tearing it apart.

How can and do individuals proceed when confronted with the dilemmas of modern society? Personal values are a starting point—a consciousness of what is, and what is not, important.

Additional tools of thought involve recognizing the patterns that recur throughout life, the simple patterns that are repeated in the complex fabric of society. The analogies between the two levels, personal and social, can offer a way to think about the most perplexing problems.

Personal and social dilemmas: the decisions we face can seem overwhelming and leave us with a sense of helplessness. Recognizing the similarities among the sorts of choices and types of problems we face can give us the confidence we need to take the first steps toward solving those problems.

The patterns that recur throughout history may be simple patterns, but they are patterns that we sometimes seem to be condemned to repeat. We will have to make some hard choices to escape the worst of fates.

Community survival rides on our choices.

There are no easy choices in a democracy. Most public decisions prove good for some, bad for others. And if group decisions are difficult, so are those of the individuals in the group.

Game theorist John Von Neumann studied one type of difficult decision, reducing it to a simple model called "the prisoner's dilemma." Suppose you and another prisoner are arrested for a crime. If you cooperate with each other and shoulder the blame together, your penalty will be relatively light. If you each blame the other person, your penalty will be more severe. The worst thing for you, though, is if you cooperate with your partner but he sells you out by blaming you for the crime.

What should you do? Is it better to cooperate with your fellow prisoner or to act in your own best interest and put the blame on him?

Acting in your own interest without regard for the other person might work once. But if the dilemma is repeated, you will probably be better off cooperating.

And yet, it gets more complicated than that. You might, for example, want to adopt the strategy termed "tit-for-tat." If the other prisoner blames you this time, you blame him next time; if he protects you this time, you protect him next time.

The tit-for-tat strategy was the surprise winner against other strategies in a prisoner's dilemma computer contest held in the 1980s. But things fall apart if someone makes a mistake, for then the relationship degenerates into an endless round of backbiting.

In 1991, scientists Martin Nowak and Karl Sigmund showed that what they call "the Pavlov strategy" will, over the long run, beat tit-for-tat in computer simulations. In this approach, you cooperate if, in the previous round,

One of history's lessons: a Nevada boom town. The town died when the area's natural wealth was played out.

both of you cooperated. You do not cooperate if, in the previous round, one or the other of the two of you defected.

In other words, while the "Pavlovian" prisoner will cooperate up to a point, he "has no qualms about exploiting a sucker." If his fellow prisoner is foolish enough to go on cooperating when he defects, he will go on defecting and making the other person pay the price.

Finally, if, in the previous round, you both blamed the other guy, then this time around, if you are a "Pavlovian" prisoner, you will cooperate. That may seem counter-intuitive. What it means is that, since the worst thing for you is to be blindsided by the other fellow, you will cooperate as long as that did not happen the previous time—even if the only thing that protected you was your own self-interest in blaming him!

As Tim Beardsley writes in *Scientific American,* "A population of Pavlovian individuals does cooperate and reap the attendant benefits. But a Pavlovian population has no tendency to cooperate indiscriminately. The weakness of tit-for-tat, Nowak and Sigmund say, is that mutation allows populations to become more and more cooperative, which eventually leads to an invasion by selfish 'always-exploiters.'"

Of course, the computer model does not prove that self-interest is better than cooperation. The prisoner's dilemma *presumes* that your highest reward comes from turning on the other prisoner; sharing the blame yields a lesser benefit.

Perhaps future scientific models will find other strategies for the unfortunate prisoner. But for now, it appears that in some social situations in which there is a relation between reward to the individual and reward to the group, a combination of cooperation and competition will often be the healthiest approach

Chelsea's first bridge to Boston was built in 1803. Today the Tobin Bridge links tiny (1.8 sq mi.) Chelsea to downtown Boston —at the same time that it cuts Chelsea in two, destroying many neighborhoods.

Chelsea was the site of the first naval battle of the Revolutionary War. Chelsea residents watched the Battle of Bunker Hill from one of the hills in town.

Much of historic Chelsea was destroyed in a series of fires around the turn of this century, but until recently its school district qualified as a historic site: the newest school building was completed in 1909.

A 100-year-old sewer system, a 104-year-old condemned courthouse, and a 137-year-old police headquarters made long-term capital improvements a necessity. The red brick historic district of the city is now home to more than 100 artists.

The city that refused to die . . .

Chelsea was first settled in 1624 by Samuel Maverick, who traded furs with Native Americans, including the Winnisimmet tribe. Great sea merchants lived in Chelsea and did business out of Boston Harbor throughout the 1700s.

Chelsea, Massachusetts, almost went bankrupt in 1991. The result of poverty, immigration, drugs, crime, or a corrupt local government.

When the state declared Chelsea "incompetent" and took over its government, there was little agreement on the cause of the economic and social disaster Chelsea had suffered.

Chelsea, like so many cities, has suffered an industrial decline. Chelsea, like so many cities, has absorbed successive waves of immigrants. Chelsea, like so many cities, has seen drugs and crime make street life dangerous.

According to state-appointed Receiver Harry Spence, who was charged with bringing Chelsea back from bankruptcy, Chelsea was caught between polarized cultures—with the governing of the city left to the corrupt.

A few years ago there was a chain-link fence around Chelsea's city hall. These days, Chelsea is a hotbed of community activity as it attempts to rebuild. Residents who have chosen to stay and fight for their community know that development of economic and social capital is essential for their survival.

Former State Receiver Harry Spence. His social theories include:

The Tinkerbell theory of democracy: "Everyone has to believe and then clap their hands."

The liquid assets theory of economic development: "A rising tide floats all boats."

its people care and create a future.

Abraham Lincoln spoke at a reception in Chelsea's Bellingham Home, built in 1659. The cemetery, which was overgrown until the Boy Scouts restored it recently, is the final resting place of Chelsea's Civil War heroes.

"**You've got to stick your neck out if you care about where you live.**"
—TIM MCBRIDE

McBride cared enough to run for office after receivership.

"**I couldn't believe we had moved somewhere in America where we couldn't vote.**"
—HOLLY FITZGERALD, OWNER/OPERATOR OF BOATYARD BUSINESS

Receiver Harry Spence described Chelsea as an "extraordinary family place, with two and three generations living in the same block or the same house." As Jane Jacobs points out in *The Death and Life of Great American Cities,* this loyalty to Chelsea is a hopeful sign. When people stay in a troubled neighborhood by choice, which she calls *unslumming,* the "community gains competence and strength," plus the ability to accommodate immigrants "in a civilized fashion."

Jacobs sees the assimilation of immigrants as "one of the great services" of an unslumming area. "The processes that occur in unslumming depend on the fact that a metropolitan economy, if it is working well, is constantly transforming many poor people into middle-class people, many illiterates into skilled (or even educated) people, many greenhorns into competent citizens."

Fairness and diversity make a city livable. Police Chief Ed Flynn made them

In the decades prior to receivership Chelsea saw a huge influx of Hispanic immigrants—as many as a third to a half undocumented—and Asian immigrants, displaced persons, war refugees. The old Chelsea immigrants were working-class English, Irish, Italian, Jewish, Polish, many of them low income.

By 1991 this tiny city of about 30,000 people, the poorest in Massachusetts, was the only city in Massachusetts with a majority population of color. (Though the local government did not reflect that fact.) In community standoffs, according to State Receiver Harry Spence, it was the "disenfranchised facing the disinherited."

The entire community was literally disenfranchised when it was placed under receivership under a five-year

Recycling Chelsea's industrial tradition. In 1900, Chelsea was known for its junk shops. Later it was the area's scrapyard. Now it is going biotech, with state-of-the-art recycling.

plan—with no votes in local affairs, no representative city government.

Ironically, the receivership may have been the key to restoring a viable democracy in a community that has been divided by racial tensions.

Spence suggests that "it is possible for government to step out of its customary role of mirroring back to a community its own internal tensions, and instead to exercise leadership in the resolution of those tensions."

goals in Chelsea law enforcement. Police moved against visible Hispanic street drug trade and against clandestine cocaine trade in Anglo bars "to demonstrate the even-handedness of our anti-drug efforts."

Spence stated his official policy: "There is no substitute for diversifying the racial identity of police officers to ease racial tensions in a neighborhood." The police force added seven minority cops and a "low-tech" solution to fear in

the streets: community policing, patrol cars, and beat cops. Police Chief Flynn says he would like to see two things: No more "For Sale" signs in the city. And residents who feel safe enough they will go out and join the Little League or the PTA.

The Weed and Seed police program has cleaned up several neighborhoods—making drug arrests, hiring youth workers, providing drug treatment—but there are fewer funds for follow-up programs in the community.

A community needs a sense of boundaries and order, according to Spence. His goal was "to redefine the basic boundaries of division in the neighborhood: to identify the fundamental dividing line as that which separates the community of law-abiding citizens from the criminal crowd, not that which separates one ethnic group from another."

Alliances and conflicts are fluid, not fixed, points out Spence. For him racism and separatism are equal evils. Collaboration across ethnic boundaries, Spence says, is difficult but imperative.

Under receivership, Chelsea's obsolete governmental machinery was replaced, the city workforce was reduced, and many services were privatized.

Despite a rather dismal statistical picture, Chelsea has impressed observers with its resilience. In *The Death and Life of Great American Cities*, Jane Jacobs cautions against judging a city's health only by statistics. She writes about the North End in Boston, an area much like Chelsea: "This is an old, low-rent area merging into the heavy industry of the waterfront, and it is officially considered Boston's worst slum and civic shame." But Jacobs finds a "general street atmosphere of buoyancy, friendliness and good health." She agrees with Chelsea Police Chief Flynn about the value of safe and enjoyable street life.

And before Chelsea could take back the reins of local government, the city had to draft a new city charter.

Chelsea hired several facilitators to guide the process, and it was a thorough and comprehensive exercise in citizen participation. Local citizens—from the politically entrenched to newcomers—were recruited and trained to go out and speak before community groups about the participation process. Some entrenched groups seemed to prefer receivership to having to "really get involved in working all this out," according to Liz McBride, one of the recruits. Still, public meetings drew between 300 to 400 people, with citizen activists working alongside experts to create a new charter.

The charter responds to some of Chelsea's past problems by creating a variety of effective Citizen Participation Mechanisms. As well as specific options for recall to ensure the accountability of officials and thus avoid the "closed circle of power" that kept corrupt officials in office previously.

The city hopes to escape the old traps of polarized winners and losers. New leadership and a new charter may well be the start of a new era of collaborative government for the diverse citizens of this community.

Hometowns are like family; you only get one.

Tito's Bakery, the biggest business on Broadway, run by a transplanted South American soccer star, serves as a gathering place for locals and a clearinghouse for information on various recreation opportunities. Local soccer coach Tito (a city charter recruit) is sharing grant money with a Cambodian basketball coach so they can bring the kids together for cross-cultural fun.

How does a city work?

The life of a city depends upon its citizens. In ancient times Athenians swore an oath to their city's future:

"We will transmit this city not only not less, but greater, better, and more beautiful than it was transmitted to us."

Ninth-grade students at the Rindge School of Technical Arts in Cambridge, Massachusetts, also hope to improve their city—"to design and build projects that are useful to the larger community"—when they enroll in the school's CityWorks program.

The students start by gathering information—not statistics but specifics. They first "Walk Around the Block," surveying their neighborhood. They take notes, make maps, shoot photos, make videotapes, and interview residents to write oral histories.

Students not only note what exists, but what is needed in their neighborhood. For them, a vacant lot represents an opportunity; students try to decide on its best use.

They meet with community leaders, city planners and developers, and neighbors to plan a community development project. Past projects have included a discovery museum, auto body shop, teen activities center.

Once the CityWorks crew envision a project, they draw blueprints and build models and display them at an Open House —a city-science fair with a healthy dose of visual arts appeal.

Program Director David Stephen says that many of the students are

"**P**eople who experience the city as sustaining and nurturing them are well on the way to citizenship. Their next step, if given the chance, will often be to seek ways to sustain, nurture, or heal the city.

"Healing, health and wholeness are, I am convinced, helpful ways of understanding how public life or politics might be revitalized. But no matter how powerful a concept we apply to politics, it is only a concept until it is lived. No abstraction—including health or wholeness —can capture what the city is all about. Only the city itself can do that."

—Daniel Kemmis, Mayor of Missoula Montana, and author of "The Good City and the Good Life," in *Friendly Exchange* Magazine

DAVID STEPHEN

Cambridge: How a city works

"Under the seeming disorder of the old city, wherever the old city is working successfully, is a marvelous order for maintaining the safety of the streets and the freedom of the city. It is a complex order. Its essence is intricacy of sidewalk use, bringing with it a constant succession of eyes. This order is all composed of movement and change, and although it is life, not art, we may faithfully call it the art form of the city and liken it to the dance—not to a simple-minded precision dance with everyone kicking up at the same time, twirling in unison, and bowing off en masse, but to an intricate ballet in which the individual dancers and ensembles all have distinctive parts which miraculously reinforce each other and compose an orderly whole. The ballet of the good city sidewalk never repeats itself from place to place, and in any one place is always replete with new improvisations."

—JANE JACOBS
THE DEATH AND LIFE OF GREAT AMERICAN CITIES

skeptical about how much they can accomplish in the program, but maintains that they do "get plugged in to their communities." For kids who may feel powerless, he says, this participation in their community can be a first step toward seeing themselves as "people who can affect that community and create new opportunities for themselves and others who live or work there."

New hope for an old city: young Cambridge residents are producing a new vision for the future.

How does a community define itself and preserve its identity?

American political rhetoric speaks of "the voice of the people." Diverse communities have yearned and learned to make their voices heard.

If you are part of America's deaf community—a group traditionally isolated—you have "heard" the voice of your community by watching others speak with their hands, using American Sign Language (ASL).

ASL is a distinct language, carrying its own culture with it. Deaf people say that Sign is a more direct form of communication than spoken languages. Less is hidden in social niceties.

Among the hearing, deafness is usually seen as a terrible handicap. A lot of effort is put into teaching deaf people to speak. But many deaf people resist, maintaining that Sign is their language. That speaking is an unnecessary compromise forced on them by a dominant culture.

Gallaudet University in Washington, D.C., is the world's only accredited liberal arts college for the deaf. As Gallaudet students consider the fate of the university and the future of ASL, they insist that their message be seen and heard. And they pose some tough questions for the rest of our society as we ponder the issues of mainstreaming and separatism. The difficult task of reconciling the demands of separate cultures with the need for a unified society.

Deaf people owe a special debt of gratitude to their schools. Since the early 1800s deaf history and culture have been transmitted in these separate centers, residential schools that acted as focuses for deaf life. Dormitories and deaf communities around the schools created a coherent community.

At the time Gallaudet University was chartered in 1864, its founder, Edward Gallaudet, was one of the greatest proponents of Sign in education. But after his death, Sign was kept out of the classroom, restricted to informal use. The resurrection of Sign in the past 30 years has gone hand in hand with a renewed sense of deaf culture.

"My language is me."

"The deaf feel Sign as a most intimate, indissociable part of their being," according to Oliver Sacks, who reported on "different social conventions" among signers.

"Virtually every black college has a black president," a Gallaudet professor observes. "Virtually every women's college has a woman as president."

In 1988, Gallaudet University students staged a huge protest, insisting that Gallaudet hire a deaf or hearing-impaired president. Students argued that there must be a worthy candidate among the generations of Gallaudet graduates. But it was "more than a campus uprising. It was a symbol, a primal scream," according to *The Week the World Heard Gallaudet* by Jack R. Gannon, "a significant chapter in the chronicle of the struggle for equality of civil and human rights among minority and disabled persons."

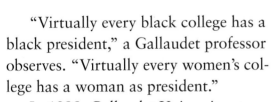

The heart of the protest over the college presidency is easy enough to see: Many Gallaudet graduates share a passionate belief that the university needs a deaf president as "testimony that deaf people are capable of leading themselves." They also want a president "who is sensitive, understands, exemplifies and advocates for the deaf, not just by rhetoric but by being a living example."

Critics claimed that by insisting on a deaf president they were withdrawing from mainstream society. By insisting on the use of sign they were creating their own ghetto.

After a week of barricades and protests, a march on the White House, and shows of support from the worldwide deaf community, student demands were met. At a victory celebration jubilant faculty, staff, and students proclaimed their triumph: "Now the university is going to be ours."

A united audience signed, "Deaf president forever!" Respect our language and our culture!

The question remains: Can the deaf culture be both separate and equal?

"The highest praise goes to the students of Gallaudet," said King Jordan, first deaf president of the university, in simultaneous Sign and speech, "for showing us exactly even now how one can seize an idea with such force that it becomes a reality." The message of community power spread throughout the deaf world.

"**W**hen I had visited Gallaudet in 1986 and 1987, I found it an astonishing and moving experience. I had never before seen an entire community of the deaf, nor had I quite realized (even though I knew this theoretically) that Sign might indeed be a complete language—a language equally suitable for making love or speeches, for flirtation or mathematics. I had to see philosophy and chemistry classes in Sign; I had to see the absolutely silent mathematics department at work; to see deaf bards, Sign poetry, on the campus, and the range and depth of the Gallaudet theater; I had to see the wonderful social scene in the student bar, with hands flying in all directions as a hundred separate conversations proceeded—I had to see all this for myself before I could be moved from my previous 'medical' view of deafness (as a condition, a deficit, that had to be 'treated') to a 'cultural' view of the deaf as forming a community with a complete language and culture of its own. I had felt there was something very joyful, even Arcadian about Gallaudet—and I was not surprised to hear that some of the students were occasionally reluctant to leave its warmth and seclusion and protectiveness, the cosiness of a small but complete and self-sufficient world, for the unkind and uncomprehending big world outside."

—OLIVER SACKS, *SEEING VOICES*

After the "transformation of consciousness" in the deaf community, deaf people went from seeing themselves as "deaf and dumb" to "deaf and able." This image change, a new sense of strength and power, had a profound effect on their community.

Speak out and break the code of silence.

Which is more important, loyalty to friends or speaking up against guns in school?

"Welcome Back to School," a sign announces. "Your Rights End Here." Fear of guns in schools has led many districts to adopt harsh gun policies, including searches.

Many guns get into school in book bags and backpacks, leading to their proposed ban in some districts. Students reply that if you want to bring a gun to school, "there are a million other ways."

"I was going to the library and I saw a stretcher go by. I didn't know there was a shooting. I was surprised there was a shooting here at Reseda."

At Reseda High, in a working-class suburb of Los Angeles, guns and violence are not everyday threats.

But on the morning of February 22, 1993, during a midmorning snack break there was a confrontation in the corridor of Reseda High's science building. A 15-year-old boy pulled out a gun and fired. A 17-year-old was hit in the chest and died instantly.

Six of the dead student's classmates knew that the murderer had brought a gun to school that day. They went to the school's principal, racked by guilt. If any one of them had reported the gun, their friend would still be alive.

Jay Shaffer, a government teacher at Reseda, thought about the students' dilemma, the issue of telling on your friends. Breaking the code of silence is a hard choice for kids who have grown up being told not to squeal on their friends.

Students and the school administration both seemed at a loss for words. Students spoke of the "shooting," not able to say "killing." The administration instituted security measures: locker searches and metal detectors.

Shaffer and a group of students started WARN (Weapons Are Removed Now). They wanted to help students think about the choices they make and how those choices create our society.

WARN develops raps and skits to teach elementary school kids that when you play with guns, the stakes are high. There's no room at school for romanticizing guns or trivializing their effect upon society.

Teens in the '90s face hard choices every day. Teachers help them learn to think and speak their thoughts.

When teens learn to tell stories or sing songs, they learn the lessons of a life lived as part of a community, of meaning and belonging. Of rituals that mark human existence, love and death.

In San Pablo, California, members of Los Cenzontles poetry workshop at the Mexican Arts Center, composed a song in honor of classmate, Cecilia Rios, who was raped and murdered in a schoolyard.

Her friends commemorated her death with the "Corrido de Cecilia Rios." The corrido is a 12-stanza epic poem set to music. Eugene Rodriguez, co-director of Los Cenzontles, says that "the corrido, historically, does not sentimentalize. It made sense for us to use Mexican traditions for the kids to express themselves."

Cecilia became a symbol as well as a loved and mourned friend:

"Fly, mockingbird, singer.
Your song will be witness
That family and friends of Cecy
Remember her with love."

In inner-city Los Angeles, teens struggle to speak about their actions.

Teen Court: *This exercise in democracy* helps teens to understand the implications of their actions. If kids at Reseda High are learning to think about the dilemmas of conscience they face each day, kids at L.A.'s Wilson High are going one step further. Learning to question their peers and plead their cases. First-time teenage offenders at Wilson High—charged with what the school considers "minor" crimes: vandalism, assault, drug possession—are tried by a jury of their peers. In a Teen Court trial—as in a Greek trial, like the trial of Sophocles—there is no evidence, there are no witnesses or lawyers. The jury questions the defendant directly. The accused tries to explain his or her actions or provide a defense.

Some teen court programs involve "good" kids judging "offenders." In Juvenile Court Judge Jaime Corrale's model program, convicted teens are sentenced to serve one day on juries trying their fellow teens.

It is an exercise in self-awareness. These kids learn to listen harder. Consider the context. Look for signs of remorse. Try to figure out what to do to help kids.

Corrale would like to have teen court in housing projects with gang members on the jury. "What we are doing," he says, "is getting young people involved in dealing with the problem of criminal behavior in the community—we're helping young people to help us deal with this problem."

Corrale's attitude is "these kids are very responsible members of our community." He has been amazed at some of the creativity the teens have demonstrated in coming up with some of their sentences.

In their evaluation of their peers, Corrale says, "They're shooting from the heart."

These markers say "Pray for me"
to every passerby.

What's Going On?

WE WILL MISS YOU, YOU WILL ALWAYS BE IN OUR HEARTS. WE'LL NEVER STOP LOVING OR THINKING ABOUT YOU. 2-8-65 5-25-94 Love Always YOUR FAMILY & FRIENDS REST IN PEACE PICHON

The words of the prophets are written on inner-city walls. Artists construct our society's collective memory. Are we learning the lessons of a violent age?

Bearing witness to pain and horror—and to a community's desire to heal itself—memorial walls all over America document the rise in violence in inner cities. These murals mourning friends and relatives who died too young speak clearly of a community's sense of loss.

"Don't forget," the murals seem to warn. Don't forget friends and neighbors. Don't forget the victims of AIDS and drugs and street crime. Every day, cities feel the knife-edge of memory that is carried on these walls.

These huge vivid murals are the *Common Sense* of the modern age. Like Thomas Paine's pamphlet, they touch a large audience—by speaking the language of that audience.

"It's like hanging a wreath on the door when someone dies," says one muralist of the walls he paints.

Candles, flowers, hearts, wooden crosses, hands clasped in prayer: traditional symbols combine with objects that indicate the deceased's interests and tastes, often revealed in mass-market products— a favorite drink, car, or cartoon character. Sometimes there are gun images, or drug and gang references.

"We draw what we want to see."

The deceased's family and friends can select the mural images, but not the dates painted below each name.

Urban tribalism. "Keeping the spirit." Some murals include a portrait of the deceased, keeping the community memory alive. Most of the portraits are close-ups

ONE OF THE MARVELS of the ancient world was the magnificent library at Alexandria, Egypt, which, thanks to its hundreds of thousands of volumes, was famous long after its destruction at the end of the classical era.

Famous, that is, among the handful of educated persons of the time. Few would actually have been aware of that grand library, for until relatively modern times learned information was accessible only to privileged classes. Today, any home computer can rival that great library in storage of information.

But at the same time that we enjoy the greatest volume of books the world has ever known, we are threatened by a rising tide of illiteracy—as schools and public libraries all over America are facing budget crises.

of faces, haunting images painted from photographs.

A source for urban rituals. Murals sometimes become the backdrop for memorial services, birthday parties, street dances. A Brooklyn elegy reads: "And though you're gone we know you're here, as we twist the cap on every beer."

Information: a weapon for democracy

KYRIE ELEISON

Government of the people, by the people, and for the people cannot work unless the people have accurate, timely, and useful information. Thomas Jefferson called information "the most legitimate engine of government."

"Educate and inform the whole mass of the people. Enable them to see that it is in their interest to preserve peace and order, and they will preserve," Jefferson said. "They are the only sure reliance for the preservation of our liberty."

Our country's founders had the wisdom to protect freedom of speech in the first amendment to the Bill of Rights. From this freedom other freedoms flow, for censorship is the first tool of repression, the first strategy of the repressor.

Today we are bombarded by a barrage of information of all kinds. Television offers us not three but dozens or even hundreds of channels. Radio provides an array of listening choices, even when we are jogging or commuting to work. Newspapers and journals on every subject, in most of the world's languages, are available to nearly all of us. The greatest research libraries in the world are accessible by computer even to people in remote areas, and through the Internet, computers also link users to an almost infinite number of sites at the touch of a few keys.

But if, for us, information is freely available, that does not mean that the information that we need will automatically reach us. As we have seen, there is no freedom without responsibility. Indeed, the greater the freedom the greater the accompanying responsibility, so that a free press requires an

"**D**emocracy," write Patrick Watson and Benjamin Barber in *Struggle for Democracy*, "is deeply rooted in talk." These roots reach back to colonial times. In the struggles of those years, "the power of the written word proved to be a weapon for democracy more potent than the sword. By the 1650s, Puritan preachers were successfully creating new and zealous converts to their egalitarian religion simply by putting books into the hands of scullery maids and manservants."

Neil Postman, in his *Amusing Ourselves to Death,* elaborates on this theme. In colonial America, he observes, "reading was not regarded as an elitist activity, and printed matter was spread evenly among all kinds of people. A thriving, classless reading culture developed....

"Where such a keen taste for books prevailed among the general population, we need not be surprised that Thomas Paine's *Common Sense,* published on January 10, 1776, sold more than 100,000 copies by March of the same year. In 1985, a book would have to sell eight million copies (in two months) to match the proportion of the population Paine's book attracted....

"The only communication event that could produce such collective attention in today's America is the Superbowl....

"The influence of the printed word in every arena of public discourse was insistent and powerful not merely because of the quantity of printed matter but because of its monopoly. This point cannot be stressed enough, especially for those who are reluctant to acknowledge profound differences in the media environments of then and now. One sometimes hears it said, for example, that there is more printed matter available today than ever before, which is undoubtedly true. But from the seventeenth century to the late nineteenth century, printed matter was virtually all that was available. There were no movies to see, radio to hear, photographic displays to look at, records to play. There was no television. Public business was channeled into and expressed through print, which became the model, the metaphor and the measure of all discourse."

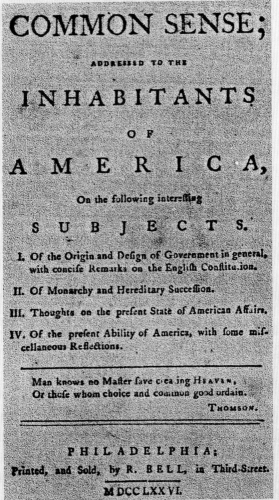

especially responsible citizenry. Too many people today sit passively in front of their television sets, indiscriminately soaking up pseudo-information filled with biases, subliminal messages, or errors of fact. The present avalanche of information means that the individual's responsibility to sort through it, to discriminate and to seek out what is needed, is greater than ever before.

Mass media has created a culture of celebrities, where not just trivial gossip about movie stars but also gossip about world leaders and the weirder elements in our midst share the front pages and the air waves. If "man bites dog" makes a better story than "dog bites man," then the stories we are offered will be the atypical and unrepresentative. "If it bleeds it leads" is a journalistic maxim. Mass media appeal primarily to emotions and only secondarily contribute to the necessary deliberations of an informed populace.

Today, candidates for election are more concerned about approval ratings than about policy. We citizens know more

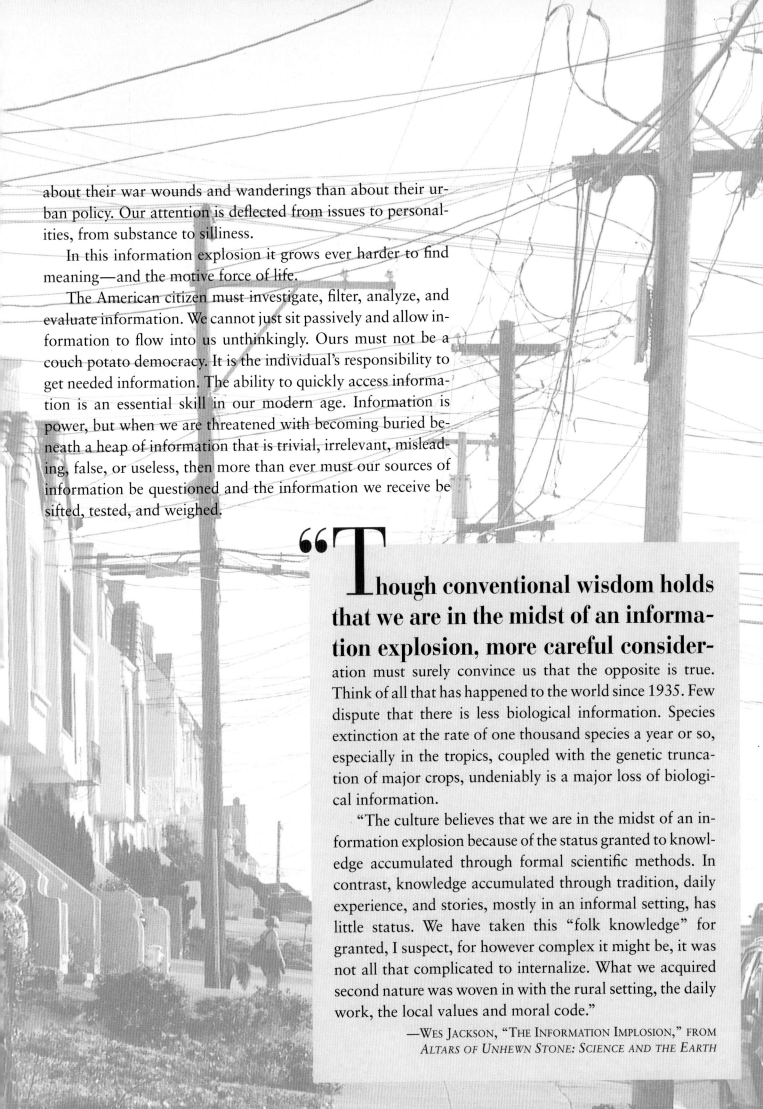

about their war wounds and wanderings than about their urban policy. Our attention is deflected from issues to personalities, from substance to silliness.

In this information explosion it grows ever harder to find meaning—and the motive force of life.

The American citizen must investigate, filter, analyze, and evaluate information. We cannot just sit passively and allow information to flow into us unthinkingly. Ours must not be a couch potato democracy. It is the individual's responsibility to get needed information. The ability to quickly access information is an essential skill in our modern age. Information is power, but when we are threatened with becoming buried beneath a heap of information that is trivial, irrelevant, misleading, false, or useless, then more than ever must our sources of information be questioned and the information we receive be sifted, tested, and weighed.

"Though conventional wisdom holds that we are in the midst of an information explosion, more careful consideration must surely convince us that the opposite is true. Think of all that has happened to the world since 1935. Few dispute that there is less biological information. Species extinction at the rate of one thousand species a year or so, especially in the tropics, coupled with the genetic truncation of major crops, undeniably is a major loss of biological information.

"The culture believes that we are in the midst of an information explosion because of the status granted to knowledge accumulated through formal scientific methods. In contrast, knowledge accumulated through tradition, daily experience, and stories, mostly in an informal setting, has little status. We have taken this "folk knowledge" for granted, I suspect, for however complex it might be, it was not all that complicated to internalize. What we acquired second nature was woven in with the rural setting, the daily work, the local values and moral code."

—Wes Jackson, "The Information Implosion," from *Altars of Unhewn Stone: Science and the Earth*

Iowa kids get a lesson in communication.

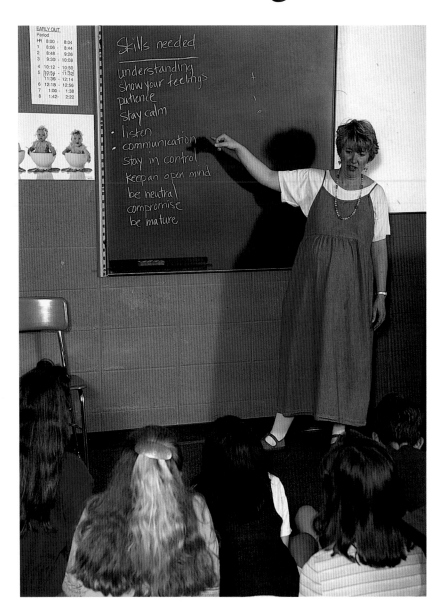

No questions, no feedback—not enough information!

In the Peanut Butter and Jelly exercise, pairs of students try to construct a sandwich. One student is blindfolded and is not allowed to speak. The other student gives instructions: the peanut butter is over here, a few steps to your left, no, too far, not that way....

Then they switch roles.

It is not a dialogue: in one role they can't ask questions; in the other, they have to keep on giving directions without verbal feedback. This is how they learn the frustration of powerlessness and the responsibilities of power.

Suddenly the kids realize that language and communication are as slippery as a jelly sandwich.

"Learn to listen."
"Talk it out. Don't fight it out."

Simple lessons. But lessons that even a child can apply to the global level.

The Iowa Peace Institute is one antidote to the "corrosive cynicism" of the mass society of the '90s.

The Institute was established by the Iowa legislature to "promote alternatives to the violent resolution of conflict."

The staffers work locally, teaching conflict resolution and mediating disputes. They also host a Global Village Program that brings together participants from around the world to "spread the news that peace is possible, that peacemaking skills can be taught and learned."

Information is a two-way responsibility.

At the Iowa Peace Institute, justice is blind. Learning to see both sides of a conflict is a matter of slipping on a blindfold.

Schoolkids who participate in the Institute's Peanut Butter and Jelly exercise enjoy learning to understand each other. If they can manage to work together, they build communication skills—and even more—they get to eat the sandwich.

Katy Otting, Director of Conflict Resolution Programs at the Peace Institute, leads the sandwich-making exercise with Diana Buter's sixth-grade Extended Learning class from Grinnell Middle School. Under her direction kids go from applying jelly to bread—to applying general principles to life.

Getting involved is "our role as public servants in the community," says editor Rick Thames, explaining why he started the *Observer*'s "Taking Back Our Neighborhoods" series.

"We can be a forum for ideas and for discussion," Thames says. "We can play a more active role in that part of the process.

"When we polled these neighborhoods [about crime], we were giving these people a voice they never really had before. It was an enlightening experience for the whole city.

"The series is an attempt on the part of our newspaper to become a constructive part of the process to solve crime. We're not going to tell the community this is what you're going to do. What we're doing is pointing out a problem and at the same time pointing a way out. Suggesting that there *are* ways to solve this problem."

Observer or participant—in public journalism...

"**Y**ou people are nothing but scorekeepers. All you do is tell us how many were killed last night." An angry voice attacks the media in Detroit.

Newspapers all around America have taken that accusation to heart. Some decided that reporting information is not enough. Activism is the answer. The news becomes a two-way street as newspapers learn to listen to their communities.

Many newspaper editors—and reporters like Billy Winn of the Columbus *Ledger-Enquirer* of Georgia—feel that if you care about your community, it is impossible to stand by passively and report its deterioration. "If you didn't *do* something, people were actually going to suffer," said Winn. "It was that clear-cut."

Some feel that taking an active role will diminish a newspaper's credibility, according to the *American Journalism Review*'s "The Gospel of Public Journalism" by Alicia C. Shepard. Public journalists reply, What credibility? Media, they say, are seen as uncaring, insensitive, and exploitative. Adherents of the fast-growing movement of public journalism have found ways to play more active roles in their communities. One strategy is "community-assisted reporting." The goal is to find out what the problems are, then to report them from the citizen's point of view.

The *Observer* of Charlotte, North Carolina, for example, prints a new kind of news. Instead of starting coverage at a city hall press conference, with "expert" quotes followed by "man-in-the-street" reactions, the *Observer* first speaks with ordinary people in local neighborhoods and only then gets the response of city officials.

"**If newspapers are just pointing out problems, we leave the community feeling this sense of hopelessness. That's part of the reason people feel so alienated by the media.**" Controversial new journalism thinks people are tired of being reminded of the problems. But they are "hungry for information. And eager for solutions."
—RICK THAMES, *OBSERVER* EDITOR

...newspapers learn to listen and keep the

Citizens are taking back their neighborhoods.

In its "Taking Back Our Neighborhoods" series, the *Observer* points out problems as the community itself sees them and then insists that the community get busy to solve them.

The *Observer* and other newspapers are trying to address problems of declining circulation and declining confidence. Problems that are inextricably linked to the communities they serve.

"In the short term," says Davis Merritt, Jr., one of the leading spokesmen for public journalism, "we're not going to solve all these problems. This has to do with the long term.

"There has to be a purpose in what we do beyond telling the news."

Scholars have studied the "disconnect" between the press and its readers. MIT Media Lab associates published *Common Knowledge*, in which they stated that "ironically the cosmopolitan and investigative style of what is usually defined as journalism at its best may reinforce [the public's] sense of powerlessness" when it emphasizes the hopeless complexity of issues. "Our subjects reacted with special enthusiasm to information about how to take control of public issues."

—Edward Fouhy,
"Renewing our Democratic Heart"

voice of the people alive.

"In thinking about voters' concerns, God is in the details....

"Anything that gets reporters out of the clutches of spin doctors and into the minds of voters should be encouraged." —Richard Morin, Washington *Post*

The *Observer's* 1992 election coverage looked to those details. Reporters asked 1,000 community residents to list the issues that mattered most to them and the paper printed an analysis of the agenda set by the voters.

The *Observer* then asked each candidate to take a specific stand on the issues selected by readers. When reporters went to press conferences, they asked the candidates questions posed by "real people." For example, "Mary Smith of Ourtown would like to ask you this question." The reporters found this awkward at first, but eventually decided it was fun—and effective.

National Public Radio, among other news organizations, followed their example. NPR Editorial Director John Dinges said, "I was very influenced by Charlotte. I wanted to do what they were doing: to let people set the agenda for the election rather than let them be led around by candidates and their handlers."

"When a newspaper picks people and places to write about," says *Observer* editor Rick Thames, "we know that they symbolize a thousand other people in the community that need help."

The purpose of the media "is to amplify and magnify people's voices and their lives, to let us all see and hear what's going on" adds *Observer* reporter Liz Chandler.

Involved journalism has brought many new voices into public life. Young people have found voice and visibility in a variety of media. Here are two:

YO!—or Youth Outlook—is a program of San Francisco's Pacific News Service, which serves 30 daily newspapers plus dozens of magazines and journals. YO! takes mostly urban and minority teens and teaches them journalism by having them write columns that offer their view of the world.

PNS Director Sandy Close is looking for stories that connect, that are intimate, that move toward the universality of experience. And she looks in nontraditional places for the writers who can tell them.

Newspapers, she says, shouldn't treat young people as an afterthought in circulation wars. They are, after all, the cutting edge of the future.

YO-TV—no connection except the youthful outlook—is a video program for students of Brooklyn's Educational Video Center. The students produce documentaries "chronicling events and concerns that are closest to home." As well as exploring new areas: they presented a full-length documentary on contemporary American art at the 1993 Whitney Biennial—a production "full of discovery, analysis, shock, and humor."

YO-TV youth leaders have presented their tapes—about violence, dropouts, abandoned buildings and what to do about them—at meetings in many communities around the country.

Throughout history, breakthroughs in information technology—writing, printing, electronics—have had dramatic impact on social systems. For information as a democratic tool, 1989 will stand as a landmark year. That was when the city of Santa Monica, California, went on-line with its Public Electronic Network (PEN), the first government-sponsored electronic network.

The system was initiated by Ken Phillips, then director of Santa Monica's Information Systems Department, and Joseph Schmitz, a doctoral candidate at the University of Southern California's Annenberg School for Communication. It began as an outgrowth of the city's internal e-mail information system. Phillips and Schmitz asked the question, Why not open the network up to the public at large?

There was opposition. City bureaucrats were leery of being a keystroke away from any citizen with a gripe or a suggestion. How would they handle the additional work? But there were also influential supporters, including the city librarian, the chief of police, and some city councilmembers.

"I found my public voice through PEN."
—JENNIFER WAGGONER

And there was great community support (one-third of Santa Monica citizens own personal computers, about three times the national average). A random survey testing community interest during the planning stages produced an extraordinary 50% response rate. In this community, people were ready for this new form of democratic participation.

Ken Phillips says, "the biggest value in any system is 'critical mass.' That is, there must be enough people on-line to make it worthwhile for you to be on-line." In Santa Monica, 1,500 users—about 1.5% of the city's entire population—may log on to the system on a typical day.

Santa Monica defined six objectives for the system: provide access to public information, improve city services, enhance communication, increase a sense of community, spread technological information, and provide equitable distribution of communication resources.

By and large the system has been successful in meeting its objectives. It has opened floodgates of communication—far more people have logged on to the system than anyone ever anticipated. Joseph Schmitz says, "What I think is so neat about PEN is that it has the potential to let people acquire information with fewer gatekeepers."

PEN's dramatic impact on the Santa Monica community has taken some unexpected turns. When access to the system was provided through terminals in public locations, homeless residents began to log on. At last, many felt, they were provided with a relatively level political

"Through PEN I have the power to affect real change in my community."
—KEVIN McKEOWN

playing field. Then-homeless Donald Paschal commented, "We without shelter are looked on with disdain, fear, loathing, pity, and hatred. This difference makes 'normal' contact with other humans almost impossible.... To me the most remarkable thing about the PEN community is that a city councilman and a pauper can coexist."

Jennifer Waggoner, another PEN user who has found a home since she began using the system, echoes Paschal's sentiments: "For a homeless person on the streets, it's virtually impossible to walk up to a city official and really express yourself in a cohesive manner in a way that they can understand.

"Before, when I was homeless, I didn't have access to any type of media that would inform me of city politics: when things were happening, and where and why. On PEN they give you meeting dates and agendas. All of a sudden I started seeing homeless issues on the agenda—closing down the parks, stopping feeding programs. Things that really said to me, Wow, I'd better get involved now, or else."

Also through PEN, concerned citizens have produced new social services that have turned homeless people into productive community members.

Not that there haven't been problems. As with any public forum, counterproductive voices disrupted dialogues and debates. Insults and threats were traded. Demeaning sexual comments appeared.

In the face of such abuses, some public officials stopped participating. But city councilmember Bob Holbrook stands firm. "There are four or five

> ❝We probably have the highest turnout of voters in the state. I think that speaks well for democracy here. And it has to do with PEN.❞
>
> —CITY COUNCILMAN BOB HOLBROOK

"PEN is like an electronic town hall," Holbrook says. **"You can access it from home or any of the public terminals that we put in around the city. You can send messages to the city councilmembers or any number of city staff—police department, fire department, places like that—just to get information. You can post things on bulletin boards, ask questions, receive answers, give movie reviews, book reviews."**

. . . can be a powerful tool for information

"Who's going to hire someone who smells?"
—DON PASCHAL

One of the most effective and innovative programs to emerge from Santa Monica's Public Information Network is SHWASH-LOCK, a city facility designed to assist the homeless. The acronym stands for SHowers, WASHers, and LOCKers, all of which are provided to homeless persons to help them get off the streets.

Soon after Santa Monica provided public on-line access to government, homeless persons began to complain about the lack of essential services. As then-homeless Don Paschal put it, "Who's going to hire someone who smells?" Soon a group of PEN users worked out practical solutions to the problem, among them SHWASHLOCK. PEN gave them the means to re-fine their ideas and put their proposals on the table for pub-lic action, and it provided the network to follow through and get them implemented. Now it is the entire community that benefits.

"You have a locker, you stay clean," says Darrell Towler, who now sees hope for getting off the streets. "It gave me the incentive to go start looking for work."

people on PEN who will flame anyone who is an elected person," Holbrook says. "It gets a bit terrorsome." Still, Holbrook praises the service. "I love the interaction with people—new peo-ple, strangers, people with a different point of view than I have, different values, different philosophies."

Ken Phillips warns, "The issue of free speech is a really important one that a government that runs an on-line network could get hung up on. What does 'free speech' mean? Does it mean that anyone can say anything at any time on any subject in any place?"

Now PEN is experimenting with stricter guidelines for participation. Participants must keep their comments to certain length limits. There are also frequency limits: the same individual cannot log on to the same topic over and over, dominating the conversa-tion and killing discussion.

"I think we'd be okay on PEN," says Kevin McKeown, a long-time user and critic of abuses of the system, "if we applied the same rules we normally apply in public meetings.

"The freedom is won-derful. But any freedom carries with it a responsi-bility. If freedom is taken to an extreme, then it can impinge on the freedom of other individuals."

But when a community is as involved and as creative as Santa Monica, then successful compromises can be found

Democracy "seems to prefer talk to force, deliberation to whim, good reasons to powerful arms, consensus to conflicts, peace to war, cooperation to competition. But no sooner do we define democracy as 'reasonable discussion' than someone reminds us that it can mean the politics of conflict as well as the politics of co-operation: or that through the power of today's media, the government of public opinion we call democracy can enthrone whim rather than deliberation.

"Democracy is not tidy. It is a rough, obstreperous, messy form of political life. Montesquieu, that thoughtful and ingenious French predecessor of both the French and American revolutions, observed that where you find an orderly silence, there you will find tyranny. Wherever we find spirited voices raised in debate, where there is tumult and faction and unceasing talk, where men and women muddle their way to provisional solutions for permanent problems—and so clumsily do for themselves what tyrants or bureaucrats might have achieved much more neatly and efficiently for them—there we can be assured that we are on the precious turf of democracy. Because democracy is finally—more than any other form of government— about people, just plain people. To be democratic is to disagree about what democracy is."

—BENJAMIN BARBER AND PATRICK WATSON, *THE STRUGGLE FOR DEMOCRACY*

Just say YES! Youth keep group alive by learning to read the signs of agreement

One on one. Face to face. That's how most democratic action happens. Youth for Environmental Sanity (YES!) is the very antithesis of the impersonal isolation made possible by technology, and the irresponsible computer communication known as *flaming*.

In our image-conscious age—an age of performance art and fashion statements—a dramatic group of environmental activists have rediscovered the basics. They take advantage of the power of the gesture to provide much-needed information.

YES! co-founder Ocean Robbins describes the Santa Cruz students who belong to the group as "people who are willing to make their lives into statements of what they believe in."

In group meetings, their actions speak louder than words: they use hand signals to smooth the discussion process. And to give each other valuable information about what is on their minds.

YES! staff choose a facilitator, a timekeeper, and a notetaker to keep their meetings on track. Members use signals that they invented to ask the

HOLE IN THE OZONE BY DU PONT

YES! does news-letters, tours, and training camps. The group organizes eco-train-ing sessions, and it also offers advice on organizational process—working together, "trying to help other people do something with their lives."

YES!'s education programs have toured over 100 cities, appearing be-fore more than 450,000 students—as well as more than 100 million people worldwide through television, radio, and newspaper stories—inspiring kids all over America to set up local recy-cling programs, eco-fairs, beach and mountain clean-ups.

The group's shows are part perform-ance, part audience participation, part organizing workshop.

"The typical high school student," says Ocean Robbins, "thinks environ-mentalists have no fun. We're showing them just the opposite."

facilitator for permission to speak. In-stead of shouting and interrupting, they use a hitchhiking sign if a member wants to make a related comment; a T with both hands to go off on a tangent; a T above head for a big tangent; hands flat out in front signal the desire to make a proposal; a finger wave says time is up; all ten fingers wiggling in the air express agreement.

Simple signals say what is important.

"The west believes that it invented democracy, and that institutions like Parliament, representation, and uni-versal adult suffrage are synonymous with democracy itself. Every American schoolchild knows that…combi-nation of electoral representation, majority rule, and one-citizen/one-vote is democracy. Because this concep-tion of democracy assumes that citizens' interests are in constant conflict, I have called it 'adversary' democracy.

"Every step in this adversary process violates an-other, older understanding of democracy. In that older understanding, people who disagree do not vote; they reason together until they agree on the best answer. Nor do they elect representatives to reason for them. They come together with their friends to find agreement. This democracy is consensual, based on common interest and equal respect. It is the democracy of face-to-face re-lations. Because it assumes that citizens have a single common interest, I have called it 'unitary' democracy.

"These two conceptions of democracy persist, side by side, in every modern democracy. The adversary ideal and the procedures derived from it have dominated Western democratic thinking since the seventeenth cen-tury. But the unitary ideals and procedures continue to influence the way legislative committees, elected repre-sentatives, major institutions like the Supreme Court, and local democracies actually act. In crises of legiti-macy, citizens often revert to the unitary ideal, as young people did in the small participatory democracies that flourished in America in the 1960s and early 1970s.

"These two conceptions of democracy are not only different, but contradictory…. Both the unitary and the adversary forms embody worthy democratic ideals, al-though each is appropriate in a different context."

—JANE J. MANSBRIDGE, *BEYOND ADVERSARY DEMOCRACY*

Is There Another Way?

C OMPROMISE, ACCORDING TO Bernard Crick, author of *In Defense of Politics,* is not just something to be tolerated, it is something to be sought. Crossing the space between my interest and yours is the first step toward creating a new direction in public policy.

Once compromise was an honored skill, the tool of statesmen, part of the art of statesmanship. In recent years, negotiation has been replaced with a win/lose model of public life— a model in which your victory may restrict my freedom and vice versa.

Deliberation is the path to the "third alternative." When parties come to the bargaining table, each with interests and agendas, the process of deliberation must create new possibilities. Decisions in which all sides "win" by seeing the welfare of the community as their shared interest and common goal represent a healthy compromise, a just *new* solution in which power is fairly distributed.

"America is a collective work of the imagination whose making never ends," Robert Hughes says in *The Fraying of America,* "and once that sense of collectivity and mutual respect is broken, the possibilities of Americanness begin to unravel. If they are fraying now, it is because the politics of ideology has, for the past 20 years, weakened and in some areas broken the traditional American genius for consensus, for getting along by making up practical compromises to meet real social needs."

"Democracy is compromise." —Saul Alinsky

"If there's *no* controversy," according to Frances Moore Lappé and Paul Martin Du Bois in their essay "Power in a Living Democracy," it means that "we probably haven't brought to the table all who have a stake in the outcome. We're only listening to those who agree with us.

"Conflict surfaces difference—the essence of public life. It brings to light the interests and values that must be incorporated if proposed solutions are to work."

"The unity of the public sphere," says the *Kettering Review,* "has been as much myth as reality," obscuring differences. When the "marginal" groups—for example, radical political organizations—become organized, new voices come to be added to the democratic process.

With diverse voices America may reinvent political discourse. Strong voices speaking out on decisions that will affect all our lives. A true public life must resonate with the voice of the people expressing themselves within a framework of reasoned and responsible discussion.

"Politics," says Ernie Cortes, "is about relationships enabling people to disagree, argue, interrupt one another, clarify, confront, and negotiate, and through this process of debate and conversation to forge a compromise and consensus that enables them to act."

We must be free to disagree as well as committed to agreeing on negotiated settlements and finding the compromises that represent society's best interests.

T he deliberations of society keep the system working. But the first step is to come to the bargaining table. "The way politics works is that once you are there, you get something," said Gary Cartwright, writing about Communities Organized for Public Service in the *Texas Monthly*. "The only people who get shut out are those who aren't there."

This is quite obviously true of a town meeting.

Our national model of deliberation is the New England Town Meeting, a 300-year-old tradition that still works in many small towns. It is a small-scale model of deliberation and compromise, research and argumentation, verbal and voting participation.

Alexis de Tocqueville commented on the lessons of democracy to be learned at a town hall meeting. He wrote that participation in its rituals rubbed off "the rust of selfishness." Participating in a town meeting is an object lesson in the way that citizens can deliberate toward a notion of the public interest, the common good.

De Tocqueville said town meetings "are to liberty what primary schools are to science; they bring it within people's reach, they teach men how to use and…enjoy it."

In a town meeting, citizens make decisions whose consequences they can actually see. There are very few spheres of public life in which this is so clearly the case.

An unusual and important series of town meetings in Pattonsburg, Missouri, illustrate the real power people have in small-group democracy. Citizens there are making decisions that they will live with for years—they are planning the creation of an entirely new town.

After the town was flooded twice in the summer of 1993, Pattonsburg received federal money to relocate to higher ground. But what kind of town do the citizens want? Can they share a vision of their future life together?

For months town residents—farmers, restaurant owners, schoolteachers, auto mechanics—have been gathering in the high school gym to sketch out their vision of a new town. They are putting their interests and ideas on the table and deliberating about the future they want to share.

Martha's Rules: The first order of business is to

Getting along with 30 adults and 7 or 8 kids is a challenge. The members of Martha's Co-op—a housing co-op in Madison, Wisconsin—would not deny that. The co-op is a small-scale democracy that faces some of the same challenges as the large-scale version.

Resident Josh Levin describes cooperative living: "When I think of democracy I think of a system that is designed to include everybody. A system that says, there's not one person or one group of people that know better and should or do have power over everybody else.

"Because our house functions as a democracy, it kind of mirrors a larger world and a larger society.

"In order to make the house run, we need policies. So we have a house meeting and everybody that wants to speak about the issue has a chance to voice their opinions. At a certain point in the meeting, we get a number of proposals on the floor, and then we vote on the proposals.

"Now the interesting thing about living in a house like this is it's a home. It's 30 people's home."

Co-op residents know full well that every individual in the household will have to "live with" every single one of their group decisions. Consensus voting —a simple yes or no, with majority rule—can be dangerous. People's real feelings and opinions can be obscured.

Jeff Haines, a sometime resident of the co-op, thought about his own feelings when presented with a proposal. He analyzed his responses and divided them into four types. The co-op then adopted his system:

Yes, I'm for it.

No, I'm against it.

I'm neutral—I'll abstain and let others decide, I just don't feel that strongly about it.

ind a way for all of us to live together.

"With challenging things, the flip side is there's always a lesson to be learned or something to be gained." —JOSH LEVIN, MARTHA'S CO-OP RESIDENT

Martha's Co-op (named for Doris Lessing's novel *Martha Quest*) is the oldest co-op in the Madison Community Co-op system. It has occupied a huge mansion on Lake Mendota just off the University of Wisconsin campus since 1969. The co-op has a dock on the lake, a garden, a communal kitchen and huge dining room, a playroom and bright living room, and three floors of single, double, and family rooms. Members share space, meals, chores, and decision making.

I OBJECT! I cannot live with this decision. Very strong words.

This last is not an option to be exercised lightly. But any co-op member can object to a proposal, which vetoes it. Other co-op members can override the veto—although that does not happen very often.

Out of respect for each other, the group works to discuss their differences, to negotiate a solution, to come up with better proposals and fewer bad feelings.

This voting procedure is called modified consensus, and it is an elegant tool of decision making, forcing residents to really listen to each other when faced with the hard choices that affect them all.

Martha's Rules work in the kitchen. "The basic community environment is wonderful," according to Josh Levin. "I like the activity. People are in and out of the kitchen...and some of them make bread. The first year, I didn't bake, I just ate it. But at some point I became a bread baker. And I really enjoy providing food for the house and doing my job, and afterward, people saying, 'Good bread, Josh.'"

A community divided. A train track cuts the town of Eagle Pass, Texas, in two. Its roads are blocked when trains stop. When they stop for hours—as they often do—the communiity is completely immobilized.

The same paralysis afflicts the town's political life. Local people—caught up in a partisan war of personalities—have lost their sense of connection, their conviction that "we are the system and we must share in the process of making it work."

Personal squabbling and political feuds—"You can't *discuss* with these people; just *'cuss,*" locals claim—have prevented the community from finding a common ground. Poverty, isolation, a poor school system, a newspaper that runs smear campaigns, all have further aggravated the problems—and further diminished the community's quality of life.

Eagle Pass residents could not agree where to build a needed new bridge. So they lost revenue it would have generated. Could not decide how to handle garbage services. So they paid to truck garbage to San Antonio.

DON WILLIAMS

Could not agree to finance a public golf course. So the fairways were left unmaintained. The town airport is dangerous. Its jail does not meet state standards. Its schools are torn by disputes over corporal punishment. A new community college gives a glimmer of hope: "It's the first project no one had anything against."

But in this culture of fighting and frustration, government is ineffective, services haphazard, and progress almost impossible. Can the government turn itself around?

Not unless citizens change their attitudes, according to Eagle Pass businessman Don Williams. When "people run for government positions," he says, "no one asks what they can contribute. It's always which side are they on?"

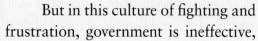

Choosing statues for

Can Americans share the town square? Can we find images and values that will serve to unify a community?

Once upon a time the statue in the town square represented—for better or worse—a community's shared past, a town's common identity.

Contemporary Americans have a more acute sense of identity, a greater sensitivity to public statements that presume to speak for them, a harder time finding a single image to represent all citizens.

The story of San Jose's search for community symbols is the story of the relationships among its citizens and the relationship of those citizens to questions of art, money, and morality. The conflict asks us to question the meaning of history in modern society.

San Jose recently found itself the twelfth largest city in America, with a large and ethnically diverse population: 37,000 African-Americans, 150,000 Asian/Pacific Islanders, 208,000 Hispanics, as well as 490,000 "others."

With a booming economy, full of civic pride, San Jose embarked upon a grand scheme to revitalize the city center. City planners rebuilt much of its downtown, creating what they hoped would be a vital urban landscape.

And then they called for art.

And got controversy.

San Jose becomes a political morality play.

San Jose City Center has had a succession of unveiling ceremonies for public art in the past few years.

The southern edge of its Plaza de Cesar Chavez was designated for a Hispanic monument. Hispanic sculptor Robert Graham created a huge Aztec Plumed Serpent for the space.

He explained his choice: "The idea of history taught in schools excludes pre-Hispanic history. It's important for people to recognize what the Plumed Serpent is—a powerful symbol. It is our heritage."

"Hispanics feel they've been left out of the new downtown, and they're right," said Barbara Vroman of the *Mercury News.*

The Plumed Serpent unveiling addressed this imbalance. Aztec dancers added music and song to downtown dedication ceremonies.

Barbara Vroman, writing in the San Jose *Mercury News,* commented on traditional public art:

> "Back where I come from, you'd never get in trouble for putting up a statue of a guy on a horse."

But San Jose did find itself embroiled in controversy about just such an image, a statue of San Jose's first Anglo mayor. Vroman says the debate "has nothing to do with art"—and a lot to do with history, "recent history, the past decade or so" of redevelopment.

If the city needed "a symbol of the work that remains to be done to make all our cultures and ethnic groups feel a part of the new San Jose," Vroman had a suggestion: an empty pedestal standing alone in the plaza.

Traditional town statues reflected the shared values of past generations. Town fathers, fighting men.

"The public sculpture of America offers a visual history of our country," says Elizabeth Broun, director of the Smithsonian's National Museum of American Art and preservation advocate.

"You have to put the *public* in public
art in order to make it work."

—JERRY ALLEN

But is it art?

Is it a work of beauty and genius? That question was scarcely considered in the San Jose art controversy.

According to legend, Quetzalcoatl was "the god who would return one day to his rightful place." Now, after much controversy, the statue has found a place in the city center.

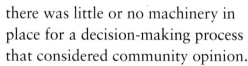

It was a charged debate over myth and symbol. Quetzalcoatl was the god of an advanced culture with an irreducible complexity. But all San Jose residents seemed to ask was: Is he "a benevolent symbol of peace and harmony" or a "bloodthirsty pagan god"? Demonic or life-giving, on your side or ours?

San Jose residents—with their grand central plaza finally taking shape—are still debating truth and history, multiculturalism and unity. And still pondering what San Jose vice-mayor Blanca Alvarado calls "the very personal, intimate ways that public art speaks to us."

"We believe public art is important for society," said David Allen of San Jose's public art program. "We don't see it as a luxury."

What better way to represent San Jose's new status as a major American city, to symbolize the diversity of San Jose's citizens, than with significant public art—an immortal symbol?

The public art program grew out of the redevelopment program. As a result, there was little or no machinery in place for a decision-making process that considered community opinion.

Then-mayor Tom McEnery had written a book about Thomas Fallon, who declared San Jose to be U.S. territory. The first statue commissioned, to be erected in the Plaza de Cesar Chavez in downtown San Jose, depicted Fallon on horseback, wresting San Jose from Mexican rule.

San Jose has 208,000 citizens of Hispanic origin. Many took offense. After a long debate, the statue was consigned to storage. San Jose was left with an empty pedestal to symbolize community values.

Next time round, the city was determined to do the right thing. A review committee was formed with representatives from the arts commission, the city

Art and money—touchy subjects both.

San Jose is a major funder of public art. According to Dorothy Burkhart, *Mercury News* art writer, "Since 1986 a percentage of the total cost of taxpayer-funded construction projects with budgets over $500,000 has been set aside for the purchase of public art." This was $3 million between 1990 and 1993.

The city cannot even reach a consensus about whether this represents an appropriate use of city funds. Despite the *Mercury News*'s argument that "great cities do great art and great social programs at the same time," some of San Jose's residents are feeling the pinch of tight budgets.

council, and a committee that reflected the city's population.

In drafting a plan for the city center, the decision process was open. There were review procedures and hearings, with testimony from activists, historians, educators, and residents.

A proposal was approved: San Jose's central plaza was to have four gateways: the north would commemorate the area's first residents, the Ohlone Indians; the east, pioneers arriving in covered wagons; the west, Pacific immigrants; the south, the Hispanic community.

A search committee selected Robert Pena Graham ,a prominent public artist born in Mexico, with ties to San Jose, to work with the city in creating a Hispanic sculpture. Graham suggested a metaphorical image, a representation of Quetzalcoatl, a plumed serpent god central to Mexican mythology.

After many more public hearings, a collaborative process in which the local community worked with the artist, an 8-foot-high, 3-ton, coiled, feathered and fanged statue was approved for the site at a cost of $400,000, plus $100,000 installation fee.

But this statue, too, proved controversial. According to David Allen, its symbolic quality made it more inflammatory than any piece of abstract art.

"In the public sector," he says, "installing abstract art is a piece of cake!

It isn't threatening or challenging. There is no meaning, per se. Abstract art does not take on social and cultural values and ideas."

San Jose's public art is not supposed to be simply art on a large scale. It is intended to be commemorative, to celebrate community values. Public art seeks to represent a community—and that is a challenge.

"The art that is most threatening, says Allen, "is the art of a community whose history is being written, because we're continually rewriting and challenging history. It's a perfect scenario for conflict."

And conflict there was—a drama of conflicting religious values.

Christian fundamentalists would not suffer this serpent in San Jose's garden. "There will be a curse upon San Jose if this statue goes up," said the local evangelical Reverend Bernal.

Protests erupted. And prayer vigils. Pat Robertson sent a video crew to San Jose and held the image up for scorn on his "700 Club" show. Despite fundamentalist wrath over what the Redevelopment Agency called Quetzalcoatl's "sublime moral sense and ethical code of conduct," the statue was erected.

But social commentators wonder, Whatever happened to *E pluribus unum*? In our fragmented society, what do we hold in common?

Planned communities—

Community planners could do worse than to consider the advice of artist Peter Fend: "What's important is a world that works, that is lovely to behold."

Planned communities throughout America have strict standards about what you may behold on their streets and in their front yards. In these towns Americans—or at least their community associations—are their neighbor's keeper.

Thirty-two million Americans live in 150,000 communities whose associations are mini-governments, private governments allowed to tax residents, unrestricted by any system of checks and balances. Community associations set strict limits on community property—regulating everything from paint to porch lights, from screen doors to mailboxes, from fences to swingsets.

The decline of natural forms of community has led to towns rigid with regulations. "Suburban utopias need rules," warns Chartwell Homeowners'

> ## "You need rules to uphold the integrity, value, and beauty of the community."
> —RICHARD HELLER, HOMEOWNERS' ASSOCIATION ATTORNEY, ARGUING CASE AGAINST METAL SWINGSETS

Association attorney Richard Heller, or "you have bedlam. You need rules to uphold the integrity, value, and beauty of the community."

To conform to these standards, the residents of planned communities are required by law to share community values, to have everything in common with their neighbors, to have nearly identical homes and streets.

Homeowner advocates say many people accept the rules of these communities less from a deep-seated desire for security and order than because there is little or no other affordable new housing available.

Other planned community residents, according to the *Wall Street Journal*, are "attracted by the strict standards, believing they enhance quality of life." It is a retreat from the disorder of modern cities, a retreat from diversity.

"It's like a tacit conspiracy between developers and public officials to privatize development of public services without admitting they're doing it," according to Evan McKenzie, professor and author of *Privatopia*. "To some extent," he says, "they are seceding from urban and suburban America."

can values be legislated?

This retreat from problems is not new. "The ideology of exit is very powerful in America," says Ernie Cortes (discussing Albert Hirschman's *Exit, Voice, and Loyalty*). "The nation was settled because of it, expanded westward because of it, and views upward social mobility as one of the most valuable expressions of it. 'Love it or leave it,' is a uniquely American expression, one that is embraced more and more frequently as citizens retreat into the walled security and complacency of the suburbs and enclaves. [The] 'secession of the successful' is a particularly apt description of the migration into suburban enclaves which have private security forces, private schools, and private recreation areas....

"The alternative to the exit mechanism is that of voice—designed to bring about change through internal agitation." Not too surprisingly, planned communities often have a problem with neighbors who raise a dissenting voice.

Despite the much-ado-about-nothing quality of these disputes, the parties deliberating over paint, pavements, and private property are embroiled in a long-standing political controversy—

the debate over whether we should protect our liberty and security *through* strong government. Or protect our liberty and property *against* strong government.

It is a question of individual freedom and community limits. With standards to be negotiated locally.

It is not the great library at Alexandria. But "America's smallest library," a five-by-six clapboard building housing some 2,000 mostly paperback volumes, is pretty important to the rural residents of Back Valley, Tennessee. "I don't know what we would have done without it," says May McGlothin, who contributed the lumber used to build the small structure four decades ago. Even the most traditional communities face hard decisions. Sharing information helps communities deliberate.

To preserve wild and also civilized life,

There are many issues involved in the argument over wolves in Yellowstone. "It's about the control of the West," says Renee Askins of the Wolf Fund. "Control and change."

In public hearings in Washington, D.C., and the West, she has been saying for years that people and wolves can coexist, but that it is necessary for people with differing opinions about the animal to learn to coexist first.

After 15 years working to reintroduce wolves to Yellowstone—the "struggle and pain" of trying to reach common ground on an issue of such "social, political, biological, and cultural complexity"—she has learned much about the way people deliberate to arrive at a decision on an issue. Askins says:

"I have learned that reason alone is insufficient to move the will. That in order to enter into the dialogue of democracy, we have to be moved by a passion.

"Part of my own personal evolution has been the process of discovery that my own passion and love for an issue has got to be a part of my own educational efforts. As a scientist, I used to feel somewhat compelled to just present the objective scientific information. I no longer feel that way.

"One of Wordsworth's lovely lines from a poem called 'The Prelude' was 'What you have loved others will, and you will teach them how.'

"I think that it is fundamental to the process of learning that we respond to people. And that people who care about something and convey that they care are probably the best teachers.

"So that my own responsibility has been to be honest about the fact that I do feel passion and at the same time to inform that passion with the most factual and accurate information that I can.

"And also to honor that other people have passions…to feel compassion. To truly listen. I think that has been really important in my work."

RENEE ASKINS

Yellowstone Park. Our first national park, was preserved more than a century ago. Now it is the site of another experiment in preservation. Ecologists are rewriting "How the West Was Won."

After years of controversy, gray wolves are being reintroduced into Yellowstone Park. Wildlife biologists hope the park will eventually sustain a pack of at least 100 animals.

Ranchers whose land lies just outside the park believe these predators have no place in settled areas. Traditionally, they have violently opposed the wolf reintroduction project.

Twelve million dollars worth of studies, more than a hundred public hearings, and comments from 160,000 people formed the basis for negotiating this difficult effort to restore ecological balance to the Yellowstone area and reach a compromise that both sides of the wolf dispute could accept.

Ranchers opposing the wolf recovery program portray the dispute this way: a bunch of city people with "warm and

can we face our most primal fears?

fuzzy feelings" about wolves, versus the steely-eyed Westerners who actually have to deal with predator attacks—the chewed-up lambs, cattle with throats slashed—as well as the loss to their livelihood.

But ranchers' voices have dominated the controversy for too long, says Renee Askins of the Wolf Fund, which led the fight for wolves in Yellowstone. "The livestock industry's cry of economic loss has eclipsed the cost of not having wolves."

Crying wolf in the West has long produced a blend of cowboy tales, ecology, and mythology.

Wolves are top predators in the food chain—a position that gives them a certain glamour among environmentalists. Combining dominance and affection, loyalty and agression, wolves are more

"Wolves Knocking on Ranchers' Doors" ran one newspaper headline. Scare tactics were used by wolf foes. "Shoot, shovel, and shut up" is how many ranchers describe their anti-wolf tactics.

Last winter wolves were captured in Canada, equipped with radio-control collars, and moved to Lamar Valley in the northeast corner of Yellowstone. Wolves were held in acre-sized pens for a few months to acclimate them to their new home. Biologist Mike Phillips expects released wolves to settle and breed in the park.

than just a popular icon for the call of the wild.

Wolves dominated the North American landscape before humans arrived. They were eliminated from the Yellowstone area early in this century. After bison were nearly wiped out and wolves began to threaten cattle in the area, wolves were poisoned, shot, and trapped in government-backed programs.

Today there are only about 2,000 wolves—down from last century's 2 million—in the continental United States, most of them in Minnesota, the only one of the lower states in which they are not an endangered species.

The wolf decline disrupted the balance of predator and prey throughout the Rocky Mountains. Today deer, elk, and moose populations are close to an all-time high, approaching the bearing capacity of the land.

Because of the wolf's major role in the Yellowstone ecosystem, wildlife biologists have been studying the possibility of reintroducing wolves into the park for the past 20 years. They expect the presence of a breeding population of wolves to have tremendous impact on the park's ecology: wolves will compete with other large predators, reduce the

PRO-WOLF SPEAKER:

"We need the silence of wild places and the music of the wolf."

size of prey populations, and affect the health of small scavengers. All of these will create accompanying changes in the area's vegetation—a reduction in the elk herd, for example, would mean an increase in the plants they like to eat—and even in the area's soil composition.

Part of the mythology surrounding wolves is associated with lone wolves—the type of wolf currently present in the Yellowstone area. The first wolves captured in Canada to be released in Yellowstone are primarily breeding pairs; they have been penned as three packs, with the expectation that each pack will establish a territorial range.

Wolves are moving back into the lower United States without the help of wildlife biologists. They are migrating from Canada into Glacier Park and Idaho. The federal biologists' reintroduction plan for Yellowstone is forcing this natural process, in part because of the special meaning that Yellowstone has for Americans, and because of its unique landscape and ecology.

> ❝**The wolf is being brought back here because it was once an inhabitant. They're bringing it home.**❞
>
> —DON TOLMAN, RANCHER (WHO OPPOSES WOLVES)

"Yellowstone," says Renee Askins, "is the only place in the 48 contiguous states that has every plant and animal species that was here when the white man arrived at our shores—with the exception of the wolf. We need one wild place that's whole. . . . Wolves belong in our oldest and most beloved national park."

For many, Yellowstone National Park is not just a spectacular and scenic park—it is the essence of American wilderness.

ANTI-WOLF:

"Coyotes make beautiful music, too, but we don't need the whole canine choir."

Which is where their opponents' fears entered in. Yellowstone-area cattle and sheep ranchers sued to block the wolves' return to the park. Their main objections: wolves would reduce the local big game population; and would soon stray outside park and wilderness areas to destroy livestock.

Two wolf plan provisions attempt to address this threat to livestock. The Endangered Species Act—which provided a legal mandate for the reintroduction of wolves—was amended in 1982 to list wolves as "experimental" rather than "endangered." This change allows ranchers to harass any wolves in grazing areas and to kill wolves attacking stock on private lands.

In another move to pacify ranchers, the Defenders of Wildlife organization has raised $100,000 to pay for confirmed stock losses to wolves. Although ranchers complain that proving claims will be difficult, the fund aims to address real rather than imagined fears.

"Time and again," says Rodger Schlickeisen of Defenders of Wildlife, "the public has overwhelmingly called for restoring wolves to their home in Yellowstone." He calls the approval of the return plan "a victory for the American people and the democratic process."

Part Three

For the People

Opportunity

Leverage

Common Ground

"...singing with open mouths their strong melodious songs."

"There can be no democracy unless it is a dynamic democracy. When our people cease to participate—to have a place in the sun—then all of us will wither in the darkness of decadence. All of us will become mute, demoralized souls."

—SAUL ALINSKY

DEMOCRACY IS SOMETHING WE do together. It is about being a member of a group, a community. Only by working together can the promise of democracy be fulfilled. The challenge democracy poses is for every voice to be raised, not in a cacaphonous babble in which everyone is speaking but no one is listening, but rather in a chorus in which we each find our part by listening to the contributions of others.

The Greek roots of the word democracy mean "the people's rule"—in the famous quote attributed to Cleon, rule "of the people, by the people, for the people." Thucydides wrote that "all that is opposed to despotic power has the name of democracy," while Aristotle defined democracy as "a state where the freemen and the poor, being in the majority, are invested with the power of the state."

But it was not only in ancient Greece that democratic processes were developed. When our nation's founders arrived on the shores of North America, they encountered one of the finest democratic models waiting for them right here. It was the Iroquois Constitution, and the colonists who framed the United States Constitution were very much aware of it.

The Six Nations of the Iroquois brought together six warring peoples—the Mohawk, Oneida, Onondaga, Cayuga, Seneca, and Tuscarora—in a peaceful confederation they called the Great League of Peace. Every five years, representatives of the member nations met to renew their bonds of unity. In so doing, they employed the principle of separation of powers: women alone chose (and had the right to recall) the male leaders, while the men whom the women chose were the

sole participants in the deliberations. Those men were allowed to keep their religion and culture, but they had to give up their tribal names. The constitution demanded that they cast aside personal ambition and individual tribal identity in order to act in the interests of all those represented in the confederacy. When a new member of the council was sworn in, he was told exactly what was expected of him: "In all of your deliberations in the confederate council, in your efforts at lawmaking, in all your official acts, self-interest shall be cast into oblivion.... Look and listen for the welfare of the whole people and have always in view not only the present but also the coming generations."

A contemporary descendant of these peoples, Joseph Bruchac, has described the meetings of the Great League of Peace that took place perhaps a thousand years ago. He has told of their practice of planting "a great pine tree as the living symbol of that green and growing union of nations." The cycle of these meetings and the growing tree that marked them represented the circles of community, the cycles of the seasons, and the future generations that the league's participants had always to keep in mind in making their decisions. As Bruchac has written: "The circle is the way to see. The circle is the way to live, always keeping in mind the seven generations to come, always asking: how will my deeds affect the lives of my children's children's children?"

We are all members of circles: family circles, community circles, natural circles. We cannot abdicate the responsibilities our freedoms entail. It is up to us to find, to nurture, and to preserve our common ground, the soil that sustains the tree of life. Only in this way can we act as stewards, preserving our world for the generations to follow.

Opportunity is the distance between what is

I Can Do It

and what could be

She'll never know if she doesn't try. Freedom and failure are inseparable companions. A young girl takes her first trapeze lesson at the San Francisco School of Circus Arts. Encouraged by her coach, with the help of other students and teachers, she faces down her anxiety, leaving solid ground behind to fly. Risk and trust, freedom and safety brought to life in a moment.

Every person, every society needs the freedom to change. Experimentation and innovation are crucial.

But change requires risk. Society depends on trust, but trust, in the form of social "safety nets," can hamper freedom as well as encourage it. Do we all need the freedom to fail?

129

...your actions can bridge that gap.

To be an American is to be an optimist. Like its music, America joins many different rhythms into a uniquely upbeat blend. Whether we arrived in this country yesterday, or our ancestors arrived generations ago, we share a faith that tomorrow will be better than today. Our children will have a better life. Anyone can be president. With hard work you can achieve anything.

Opportunity is fundamental to our idea of democracy. If we are not moving ahead, we are falling behind, failing. Traditionally, we have embraced risk, the unknown—that is where freedom lies, on the edge, on the frontier.

America has always waved the flag of opportunity. For G. K. Chesterton, the American belief in opportunity was like a national religion: "America," he said, "was the only nation in the world that was founded on a creed." That creed, writes Don E. Eberly in *Restoring the Good Society,* "consists of many things: the uniquely American idea of progress and special destiny, equality, liberty, optimism, and boundless opportunity."

Scattered, chaotic, uncertain, and prolific as it is, the free market, with some checks, has created our way of life. It has fueled a society of great material wealth and unparalleled choice. It has propelled us forward. It is flexible, fast-moving, and forgiving. It has generated thousands of failures and bankruptcies, to be sure, but it abolished debtor's prison and welcomed the failed businessperson back into a productive role.

"Choose any American at random," said Alexis de Tocqueville "and you will find a person of burning desires, enterprising, adventurous, and, above all, an innovator."

"A new social order has evolved that started with a reliance by citizens on government for the solution to certain economic, social, and cultural problems and has grown to include pressures on government to mitigate almost every risk any individual might be asked to bear.... The movement is away from a reliance on the rational individual as a decision maker and a bearer of the consequences of his choice to a socially determined allocation and distribution of resources, much of which is designed to shift the responsibility for both new and existing risks from individual to society....

"People will continue to count on the great answers, the miracle breakthroughs, and the single equitable solutions. One can only hope that these dreams will not end in totalitarian solutions; that a place will be left where each individual can dream his or her private dreams; and that eventually people will learn to accept the inevitable, achieve the possible, and tell the difference between the two.

"In fact, in the coming age of humility, there should be a healthy skepticism toward "one and only" answers. To live in an interdependent world, a moderate balance must be struck between private rights and social obligations, between individual freedom and societal restraint."

—YAIR AHARONI, *THE NO-RISK SOCIETY*

But opportunity is more than markets. It is the underlying values that matter: choice and second chances. Capital and social capital build our society. It is a tricky balance: if our choices are too safe, we remain locked in the status quo; if they are too risky, our losses are likely to exceed our gains.

The irony is that when we think too big, we lose the confidence we need. Most opportunities are small and close to home. The future arrives one day at a time. Businesses are launched one dream at a time. Sweeping reforms start up-close and personal.

Where are tomorrow's opportunities?

S ometimes one person capitalizes on the opportunity America gives each individual to be original and creates a wealth of choices for all of us.

In China 100 million bicycle riders have only one choice: clunky black Penguin bikes. A generation ago, Americans had two choices, the paperboy Schwinn or the sleek English racer.

At that time the bike market was flat. Then a bunch of hobbyists in California created a billion-dollar market in new bikes: racers and road bikes, stump jumpers, trail bikes, hybrids, and tandems. In 1993, 8.4 million mountain bikes were sold in the U.S. Now hundreds of companies and untold thousands of one-person shops are producing new and better mountain bikes.

Ask the dreamers.

Bikes are not just for transport anymore—all because one rider dreamed of riding where no one else had gone before.

The father of the mountain bike, Gary Fisher, shows off the first mountain bike he created. Fifteen years ago, Fisher, bike racer and bike mechanic, took the classic heavy Schwinn bike and went barreling down mountain trails for the thrill of it. To that bike, Fisher added the multiple gears of a racer so he could go uphill too, and the sturdy fat-tired trail bike we know today was born. He was not out to change the world or make a million dollars—but he ended up, he says, "making money despite my best efforts."

Fisher just wanted the freedom to go off-road under his own power. He blazed his own trail and set a whole new industry in motion.

GARY FISHER

"I'm going to put together something that will be able to ride up the hills, down the hills, go relatively fast, really fast, the fastest, and do it day after day, week after week...again and again."

Now he says, "The original idea was great, but now I think, what's next.... The excitement is making life better."

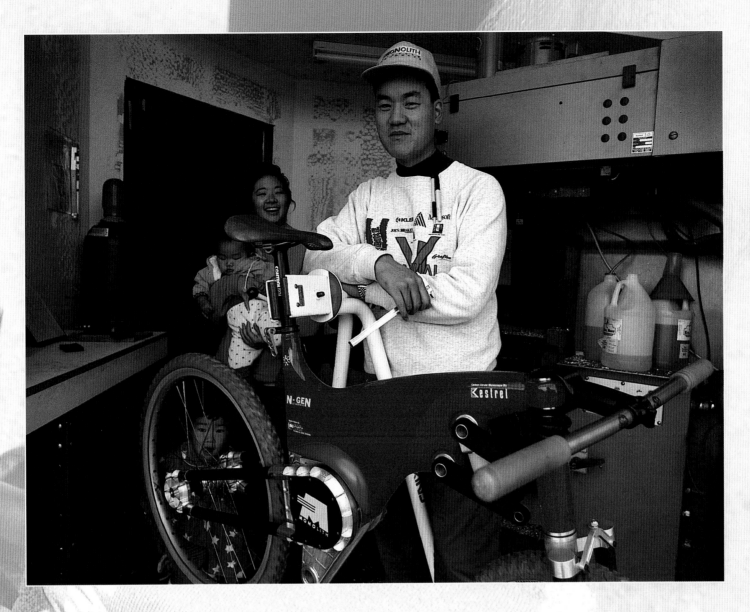

The tinkerer, the garage inventor...every entrepreneur working on a dream.

For Spencer Owyang, bike designer for Monolith bikes, it is a dream of "art and design," the desire to make the "bicycles of my passions." Owyang says he "needed to create this bike, because this was really the accumulation of where all my thoughts about the way bikes should be done drove me."

In his quest to create the "Next Generation Bike," he has a "real good support staff"—his wife, "who has just been a trooper" and his family. "Here we are,

four years into the bike venture and we've got huge debt and the thing's not turning big bucks. But I've always felt that we're right on the threshold there, and that's what has always kept us going."

The opportunity to dream and build on that dream has taken him down a rough road, and yet he perseveres. "I truly believe that I fear failure much less than most people. I would never have gotten this far, I would never even have started this thing if I really worried about it too much."

Brooklyn: the final frontier. The Hip Hop Bank launches bold new urban enterprise.

"All you need is a heartbeat and 10% to get a chance."

—LOAN OFFICER BILL WILKINS

"**F**inancial empowerment is for everyone in a free society." In an era of redlining and service-fee greed, the Hip Hop Bank was founded to bring trust and cooperation to lending in Brooklyn.

Errol Louis and Mark Winston Griffith, founders of the Central Brooklyn Federal Credit Union (the "Hip Hop Bank"), believe the power to participate in a democracy is directly linked to the distribution of assets in society.

Griffith says, "We are basically community activists from the hip-hop generation who decided it was time to resume the work of the civil rights and black power movements. We believe that building community-owned economic institutions is the final frontier."

They were bankrolled by the very banks that would not lend in the neighborhood. The big banks reasoned that Griffith and Louis knew the neighborhood and could judge the risk better. It is the kind of knowledge you can take to the bank.

Hip Hop's Youth Empowerment Program does outreach and arranges youth internships, training leaders and building new community institutions. "We're not recruiting 'young bankers' in our community," Angela Riley, the Youth Empowerment Program director, explains. Instead the program seeks to make average community members more fiscally aware. After all, "everyone has a relationship with money."

"Financial literacy" is the goal, says Riley. "We need to address this belief—that the only way to get rich in Brooklyn is to win the lottery."

Locals are taking advantage of the opportunity to secure personal and business loans. Membership in the Credit Union has gone from 30 new members a month to more than 200. The joint is jumping; and so is the newly revitalized neighborhood.

"When you give, you get back." That is the beat the Hip Hop Bank is taking to the streets.

Griffith and Louis, both inner city kids who earned Ivy League degrees, are members of the hip-hop generation. The two, Louis explains, "do a lot of what hip-hop music does, which is to take bits and pieces of the past and put it together in ways that can be innovative." Witness Griffith's opening-day remarks at the Central Brooklyn Credit Union, April 16, 1993:

"I'd like to begin by giving props to all my credit union homies in the house who've been dropping loud science from jump; by giving a shout-out to all the bankers and funders from Money-Makin' Manhattan, and by saying peace and givin' 'nuff respect to the 'Ville, the 'Bush, the Fort, Do-Or-Die Bed-Stuy, Crowning Heights and the entire Central Brooklyn posse. Peep this: We're 'bout to take it to ya face...

"In other words, ladies and gentlemen, I'd like to introduce you to the world's first hip hop credit union. Now, before you start inching towards the door and cancelling your deposit checks, let me explain. Because your understanding of what I mean when I seemingly talk in tongues and refer to Central Brooklyn FCU as a 'hip hop credit union' is critical to your understanding of the Central Brooklyn Partnership's larger mission.

"Think of it. Rap music takes beats and riffs largely from the '60s and '70s, the glory tears of uncompromised pride and hard-driving funk and black power consciousness.

"The ideals of that period constitute the beat, the riff, over which today we superimpose new lyrics and themes that express our present condition. The present reality is that locally we have finally achieved total local political representation, at least in the form of black elected officials. We have finally achieved cultural self determination—dreadlocks and kente cloth are virtually the norm. But, arguably, the people of Central Brooklyn have less power today than ever been before. And the worst part about it is, people my age and younger, those who are part of the emerging post civil rights generation, those endowed with the anger of the black power movement and dreams of the civil rights movement, can barely even imagine what real economic empowerment looks like, much less how to practice it.

"And so that's what a hip hop credit union is all about...what it means to be a black owned financial center. With the same poetry and improvisation of today's quick tongue artists, we are going to have to find ways of innovatively leveraging the indigenous wealth of North America's largest black community and help reshape it in our own image, on our own terms.

"Peep this: This time, we're taking no shorts.... Bring the noise! We're 'bout to take it to ya face.... Peace."

An open and shut case for opportunity:

"Silicon Valley is a haven for people like me. Anything goes. No punishment for failures. Color, difference, gender, it's much more forgiving."

—PAULINE LO ALKER

"The American system—it's open to all kinds of ideas, open to opportunities for all different people. If you ask me to think of one quality about this country that enables people to create value and contribute to society, it's the openness."

So says Pauline Lo Alker, Chinese-born CEO of Network Peripherals, a thriving computer-network products business in the heart of California's Silicon Valley. A company with 43 employees and annual sales of more than $20 million, it makes adaptors that speed up computer communication.

"I am a global business person. I love it," says Alker, who moved around the world and then moved up through the ranks of several American companies before starting her own.

Born near Canton, she was in two wars before she was seven years old. "It was hard for a girl back in those days in a Chinese family; it is very much a male-dominated society. And traditionally, "being born to the wrong family, the wrong name, or a family with no assets" carried a stigma. By the time she attended "the wrong high school" in Hong Kong, she knew she

"This country has given me opportunities. I want to create opportunities."

—PAULINE LO ALKER

would "be handicapped when [she] graduated," relegated to a minor civil service job.

"Fortunately," says Alker, "I had a dream. Ever since I was small I was a movie fan." From that exposure to American culture, she concluded that "in America nobody would care whether I came from a wealthy family or not. All that would matter was keeping up with the rest of the American kids."

She got two scholarships to Arizona State University to study mathematics and music. She learned the news only after discovering that her parents were hiding the acceptance letters she had

Silicon Valley and Koreatown

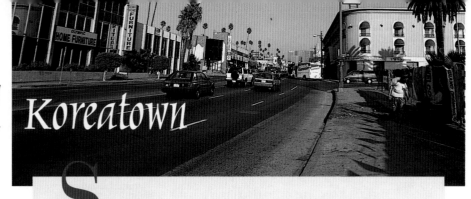

received, because they did not want her to "overshadow" her brother.

When she earned her degree from Arizona State, she wanted to be a computer programmer. She sent out 60 job applications. Not one reply! She couldn't even get an interview. "It shook my confidence and my belief in the American dream quite a bit," says Alker. But she didn't give up.

Finally she got a typing job with General Electric. And what she learned was "very important. There is no shame, if you can't go through the front door, then go through the back door." It worked for her. She quickly moved to a programming job. She never had a marketing or business class. Her career moves were "intuitive, not analytical." She has never looked back.

Social capital can be built on trust and tradition, a solid foundation of cultural constants that bind a community together. In the Korean-American community in Los Angeles, the *kye* (the word is an adaptation of a Chinese character meaning solemn promise or bond), or community lending circle, raised the money to start thousands of small businesses—and create hundreds of millionaires—all without help from mainstream banks.

When Korean immigrants first came to the United States, they found it difficult to obtain money from banks, so they turned to their traditional money-lending source, the kye. A kye is a small group of trusted associates, sometimes friends or relatives, who agree to meet for a specified period of time. At each meeting, often over a shared meal, each member of a ten-person kye puts in a certain sum of money, say $5. One member collects $50. At the next meeting, the same procedure is followed and a different member collects the money.

Since their introduction in the U.S., kyes have grown bigger and are now organized by professionals. Members now sign contracts, and in some kyes they are expected to put in thousands of dollars each week. The rules have grown more complicated, too. Members can bid for the chance to get the jackpot, in cases where the money is needed right away.

It is a common tale of immigrant life. Each group brought its traditional culture, which provided social capital, the ties that held the community together. This created opportunities for the immigrants in their new country. But as each group realized its dreams, some of the traditional systems have failed. Recently kyes have been a target of criticism; some kye organizers have been charged with fraud, one court declared the kye an illegal lottery. Lending circles have worked for centuries in many different cultures, bringing together friends and villagers. Can kyes work in a mobile society, a society of strangers?

American vets—the long way home

Sometimes opportunity is a helping hand—or a vision of justice. Ken Smith thought the Veterans Administration was not doing enough to help Vietnam veterans who had become outsiders in our society. He started the New England Shelter for Homeless Veterans. Opening doors to veterans who are getting a second—or a third, fourth, or tenth—chance at finding their place in the world.

Within the shelter's structure vets move up through the ranks—a vet might go from a detox bed one month, through training, and eventually become company commander, TV man (who gets to decide what everyone watches on the single TV), the MP at the gate, or the Officer of the Day—or even walk out the door to a job interview wearing a donated designer suit.

"All these guys ever wanted was to come home. It's time they did."

—KEN SMITH

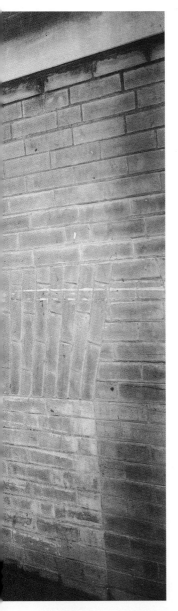

Ken Smith is not one to wait until opportunity knocks on his door. When he decided to create a program to return homeless vets to society, he went out and started knocking on doors himself.

"Let's do theater," he said. "The Greeks put on theater. It was originally developed to teach society about issues. It's a program designed around a form of democracy."

So he approached playwright David Mamet, who wrote a fundraiser, "Sketches of War" for him. Performed by actors like Al Pacino, Christopher Walken, and Donald Sutherland, it raised $250,000.

Armed with that success, Smith walked into a congressional committee hearing and talked them into giving his project an abandoned Federal Reserve building "smack in the heart of downtown Boston."

It may be Boston, but it's no tea party. Sandbags and MPs block the door, where residents are frisked, told to remove sunglasses, surrender all meds (prescription drugs), and sign in. Twenty-four hours a day, penalty boxes and counselors for backsliders are only a phone call away.

"The army makes men; we remake them." —KEN SMITH

Smith—who, before he decided to reform the bureaucracy, went from Rhode Island altar boy to adventurer in Colombia and Angola to paramedic in Vietnam—might not sound much like Gandhi, but his program dedicated to enabling vets themselves to "carry our wounded" has reclaimed many lives torn by violence.

Shelter residents say the neighborhood—City Hall, banks, the State House—"gives us something to compare ourselves to, something to give us a notion of where we need to go."

Veterans won over neighborhood support by establishing a security program. "We care," says Smith. Former military police patrol the neighborhood 24 hours a day, 7 days a week. Shelter residents get out and sweep the street once a month and do outreach and homeless intervention on their block.

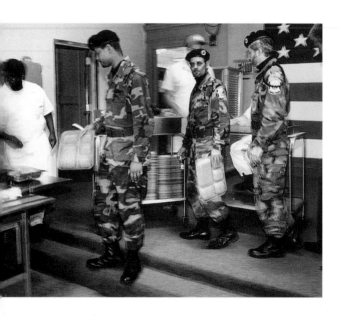

Survival skills—the shelter encourages innovative supply acquisition. The vets beg, barter, and broker enough food to serve 250,000 meals a year. With all this food preparation, a culinary arts program is in the works.

"Every man in this place has at least one thing going for him," says Smith, **"that enormous pride he felt the day he left boot camp as a soldier. I appeal to that pride. I bang 'em over the head with it." The result is a spit-and-polish barracks, bunks made up so tight you can bounce a dime off them.**

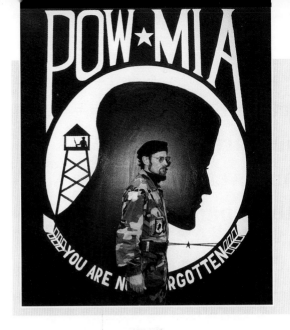

"Some of the vets were so badly damaged in 'Nam, they'll be with me till the day I die," says Smith. But others get on their feet again. "Get their act together. That's what it's all about. And then get the hell out of here."

The shelter's motto promises that it is "Taking care of business: turning homeless veterans into taxpayers."

That is no an easy job. The shelter builds on the security and familiarity of military routine to return structure to the veterans' lives. There are strict rules—no drinking, no drugs, no excuses. Of the shelter's 50 employees, 43 are vets. Their departments are set up military style—mess, supply depot, laundry, etc.—but the men who run each department have the power to make a lot of their own decisions. Still, as one vet explains, "They *have* to have a lot of rules. The rules are made for people who have not had any rules for a while. The rules keep you straight and they keep you focused."

And they help build "a feeling of teamwork," as the vets are required to volunteer time each week to maintain their shelter. The program is building social capital: vets have to get together and invest in what they all believe is important to get anywhere in life, to make any kind of economic progress. Smith says, "It's not warehousing. It's a process that we push them through."

Vets who enter the shelter either enroll in school—as full-time students —or get a job. Smith has the network to find jobs, whether flipping burgers, mopping floors, or hauling furniture.

"This shelter represents one-stop shopping for the homeless vet," says Smith. Within the compound are a barber shop, clothing supply depot (with a hundred tons of donated clothing each year), medical services, an eye clinic, Social Security and legal services, employment and housing offices. The facility also provides computer training on-site and job training within the local community. A Veterans Administration (VA) outreach office, nicknamed Fort Apache, has even opened in the shelter, with five full-time staffers giving vets access to traditional VA services and programs.

Shelter veterans have a "town meeting" every Monday night, and attendance is mandatory. That is where they get a chance to speak up. "We can air our gripes or say thank you." The town meetings travel about once a month; they've been to Patriots football games, the Kennedy Library, the Concert for Walden Woods. "How else," asks Smith, "can they get ready to move out into the world?"

Move out they do. More than a thousand homeless vets have passed through the live-in program—many of them traveling cross-country to take the opportunity—and more than 800 of them now have full-time jobs and permanent housing.

"The first words out of our mouths to veterans are 'Welcome home, brother.' A lot of them start crying; no one ever told them that before. No one ever honored their sacrifice or tried to understand their pain."

Psycho-social. It is a different kind of problem suffered by the Vietnam/Desert Storm vet. And a different kind of help: peer counseling, post traumatic stress disorder (PTSD) counseling, Agent Orange treatment, substance abuse treatment. The shelter provides what Smith feels society should have offered the vets: a place to belong, a place sensitive to their problems and needs. A place that can help them escape from their cycle of failure.

Smith's shelter project started when he visited the Vietnam Memorial in Washington. In its shadow he saw 40 or 50 veterans living in cardboard boxes clustered around this visible symbol of their pain.

His shelter has its own memorial wall, the names of vets who died after they came home: "Hero soldiers who died like rats in the gutter from ODs and hypothermia." His project has given them the chance to come in from the cold.

"Homeless, to me, felt hopeless," the vets say. Smith replies: "No, there is a solution, solution lies in the community-based organizations."

The nightmares of war have created a living hell for its survivors. George Mendoza, the shelter's PTSD specialist, lost family, friends, and homeland in Argentina's dirty war. From warrior to healer, he now deals with "compound fractures of the heart and spirit," as veterans pour out their rage and grief to him, in stories they have never been able to tell before.

Psychiatry, psychoactive drugs. The vets have tried these. But their trauma is finally responding to Mendoza's therapy. Smith continues the therapy. He brought a North Vietnamese soldier to one of the shelter's town meetings:

"It was very powerful and it was very emotional. But it was also very healing. Some vets were very angry at me. But I thought it was a very important step, a very bold step to take so that both of us could begin to express ourselves and establish some dialogue about what it was that we felt. The anger and the frustration. And the same for him."

Mendoza says, "I think that with the process of healing Vietnam veterans we are going to heal our society." Honor, dignity, trust, all need to be restored.

Veteran Robert John Byansk, Jr. points to his buddy's name on the memorial.

Strengthen your voice and you're more likely to be heard.

Social capital is a term to identify the value of a community's relationships, the time and energy people have for each other.

How do you measure the social capital or public health of a community? Studies have shown that there is a direct correlation between the number of choral groups in a community and community health and vitality. Robert D. Putnam, in his article "The Prosperous Community: Social Capital and Public Life," observes that "members of Florentine choral societies participate because they like to sing, not because their participation strengthens the Tuscan social fabric. But it does."

Rebecca Rottsolk is doing her part in Seattle. Since 1982 she has been directing the Northwest Girlchoir, building it into a national model for performance-based music education.

Rottsolk started at the individual level, giving the girls of her community the opportunity they needed, teaching them to sing, and enabling them to come together in a group that has inspired their community.

Add your voice to others
—a chorus of different voices—
and you can make a difference.

The quote at right is from Mary Catherine Bateson, *Peripheral Visions: Learning Along the Way*. Learning how to work together, girls help shape their futures.

"**Perception, attention, grace, all of these, varied or sustained, provide materials for constructing both self and world.**"

Participating girls find that being members of a group working together at a high artistic level helps them to acquire self-confidence (at an age when many girls experience self-esteem problems), to develop their individual sense of identity, and to bring into focus their personal goals and values. The North-west Girlchoir has created a future for many of these girls.

The results have been spectacular; a glorious sight and sound. "For us," Rottsolk says, "singing is a joyful occasion."

How Can We Make a Difference?

Participants in San Francisco's annual civic ritual—a marathon race through the streets of the city, in which participants range from the world's fastest runners to teams of grandmothers in caterpillar costumes—make a public statement. They are in little danger of falling into the rigid roles described by Richard Sennett in *The Fall of Public Man* as the bane of 19th-century idealogues:

"They could not play. To lose the ability to play is to lose the sense that worldly conditions are plastic. The ability to play with social life" is part of an adult public life, a life in which ordinary people can express "believable feelings clearly and freely in public." San Francisco's race favors free expression—and participation by all ages, races, sexes, however fast or slow. Thousands of people of every stripe coming together to make one grand event all can enjoy. In Bay to Breakers, as in any community-building exercise, the *process* is at least as important as the ultimate goal.

LEVERAGE IS AN AGE-OLD remedy for powerlessness. "Sometimes," according to Frances Moore Lappé and Paul Martin Du Bois, "the power of wealth or institutionalized positions appear unmovable. But they are only the most visible sources of power."

Lappé and Du Bois recommend we look to other sources of power: "information and knowledge, image, persuasiveness based on truth and reason, the impact of numbers—numbers of people and the quality of their commitment, their willingness to persevere."

These are the fluid sources of power that create a lively working democracy. Collective action builds social capital by focusing on community opportunity, the community benefits arising from cooperation.

Social capital makes communities rich—in networks, norms, and trust. So says Robert D. Putnam in "The Prosperous Community" in *The American Prospect*: "Social capital is what the social philosopher Albert O. Hirschman calls a 'moral resource,' that is, a resource whose supply increases rather than decreases through use and which (unlike physical capital) becomes depleted if *not* used. Unlike conventional capital, social capital is a 'public good,' that is, it is not the private property of those who benefit from it."

One case aptly illustrates this principle: COPS, the Communities Organized for Public Service in San Antonio, Texas (see pages 32–39). In its 20-year history of community organizing, COPS has used many of the tools of alternative power: assembling information from public records to present the city

COPS *confronted the traditional power of*

council with a budget that addressed their neighborhood needs and assembling a number of dedicated people in public actions, demonstrations by which the "powerless" of the community could make their presence felt. Their commitment, their willingness to persevere changed their neighborhoods—and their entire city—for the better.

"OUR ORGANIZATIONS," SAYS Ernie Cortes, an organizer who has worked with COPS leaders since its early years, "plan 'actions'—public dramas where masses of ordinary people collaboratively and collectively move on a particular issue with a particular focus…what the Greeks called *praxis*, the action which is aimed, calculated, and reflected upon."

At COPS house meetings, members discuss the role of a "public person" in much the same terms that Richard Sennett uses in *The Fall of Public Man*, making the distinctions between public and private person that allow the group to create (as Sennett puts it) "a sense of itself as an active force." Like religious ritual, their political action "is not self-expression; it is participation in expressive action whose meaning ultimately steps beyond immediate social life and connects with the timeless truths," sacred ideals of justice and humanity.

The public dramas that COPS enacted made San Antonio policymakers accountable. "COPS moved decisions out in the

Small change led to large. "I'm doing this because we're winning," George Ozuna's grandmother told him when she participated in the first COPS actions. At last, she said, "we have a say-so in what's going on." Ozuna is now a COPS leader himself.

money with the revolutionary power of people.

open, got them out of the back room," according to COPS' first president, Andres Sarabia. "And developed leadership. The most important thing is leadership, not the issue.

"People need to learn to act. The ability to act is power."

Mary Beth Rogers described some of the first COPS actions in *Cold Anger: A Story of Faith and Power Politics:*

"To let the mayor know it meant business, COPS targeted two of San Antonio's most venerable institutions: Joskes department store and the Frost National Bank. On February 4 and 5, 1975, hundreds of COPS members first went to Joskes, trying on everything in sight and buying nothing. Then, they lined up at the teller windows at the Frost Bank, changing hundreds of dollars into pennies and then back again into dollars. It was chaotic and disruptive, but perfectly legal. Its participants were the men and women who had quietly supported their church and community activities before without so much as a hint that they could be so disruptive of downtown San Antonio commerce.

> "We did have power, people power. And by staying focused, staying organized, and sticking together, we were able to make the changes. I like to think of it as a 'bloodless revolution.'"
>
> —ANDRES SARABIA, FIRST COPS PRESIDENT

"George Ozuna was seventeen when he and his grandmother went downtown the day of the Joskes try-on. 'When we got downtown, I saw some kind of demonstration,' Ozuna remembers. 'So I told my grandmother that we'd have to walk around. She said, "Oh, no." It turned out she was part of the whole thing.'

"While COPS members like the Ozunas were tying up sales clerks and bank tellers, other COPS leaders were holding private meetings to persuade the city's retail and banking executives that it would be in the city's best interest if they persuaded the mayor to meet with COPS on the counter budget" that COPS was proposing.

Beatrice Gallego, whose knees shook at the first city meetings she attended, now feels at home in City Hall. COPS has become a vital contributor to San Antonio's decision-making process.

"Meanwhile, television stations carried prime-time news coverage of COPS members trying on furs, shoes, and expensive jewelry and creating lines in the Frost Bank lobby, frightening away hundreds of paying customers who avoided the downtown area altogether. Retailers began to panic. Who knows what these people might do next? Something had to be done…. COPS eventually got the city's commitments for more than $100 million in improvements."

"It was a victory, but not a victory of one, a victory of many," said Andres Sarabia.

Group leverage: COPS' community actions consciously exploited its power. "The government machine was so strong," Beatrice Gallego explains, "we were literally out of their politi-

Society is a partnership "in all science, a partnership in all art, a partnership in every virtue."

—Edmund Burke

cal game. They were gaining and we were losing. We had to get united, be sure of facts and figures.

"That's when we went to the banks and knocked on the windows. We fought with business people about jobs. We went on to voter registration—single-member districts made the greatest change in San Antonio. We were no longer voiceless and faceless....

"The strength and power we have is not personal, it's organizational," Gallego stresses. "We're institutionally based. Ernie's given us good training, and also the priests and the nuns, and we're all a family, we're united, we're working together."

And yet COPS is not just "masses" of people, Sonia Hernandez says. "We don't think in terms simply of getting out numbers of people. Each is an individual, and you address people as individuals. You make sure each person has an understanding of what we are going to do and why, and what their role is."

The COPS organization knows the power of human relations. "Personal development," according to Cortes, "occurs only within a dialogue, a framework if you will, in which persons interact with each other and with their traditions.

"Institutions, be they familial, religious, cultural, or political, provide the framework within which civic education, character development, and leadership development must be nurtured."

The ongoing success of COPS depends on an awareness of the political process, constant evaluations of the effects of their actions. The process of arriving at compromise is studied: COPS members, Cortes says, learn "how to appreciate the negotiations, the challenge, the argument, and the political conversation."

COPS members have learned the everyday language of public life. And enjoy the "public goods" and revitalized community relations they helped create.

One for all and all for one—lending a

You don't let your friends down.

A few years ago, a new beauty supply store opened down the street from the one Barbara Jean (BJ) Slay owns in Englewood. Business was down, and the store threatened to go under. In desper-

ate need of a loan but too far in debt to get help from a bank, she drew together a group of old friends—all of whom were running or starting small businesses in addition to their regular jobs—and formed TeamOne, a lending circle that borrowed

and to community groups fighting poverty.

money from the Full Circle Fund of the Women's Self-Employment Project (WSEP) of Chicago. The group as a whole signs off on each loan that is taken out. No one else is eligible for a loan until three timely payments have been made.

A circle of friends. Neighbors working together. That is the start of leverage. Creating individual opportunity and building community life.

A group of friends in the Englewood neighborhood of Chicago got some economic clout when they pooled their resources. They stood security for each other to obtain loans to support their small businesses.

Small business is the essence of opportunity, and these smallest of businesses are allowing Chicago's low-income women to build new lives for themselves and their families.

Joining a group to work together builds trust—earned over time. "Social capital," along with the capital secured in WSEP loans, has created opportunities for Chicago women. Sixty loans to Chicago's low-income women have all been paid back without default.

And there is a bigger payback. Lending circles lend a hand to the community.

TeamOne is unusual in that it is made up of old friends, and no one except Slay is really depending on it for her livelihood. But that makes it strong and dynamic, a good pool of talent to draw on for ideas and sustenance. "Five minds are always better than one," these women like to say. "The concept is good, for having a business and having four other people back you and support you…four other minds thinking and strategizing."

TeamOne is known for its tight friendships, good humor, and professional attitude. "We disagree, we disagree frequently, but we make a joke out of it," Loretta Childs explains. "And we get things done because we realize the importance of getting it done."

BJ: "When people come in here, I have to sell them. I have to educate them. I have to social work them, you know."

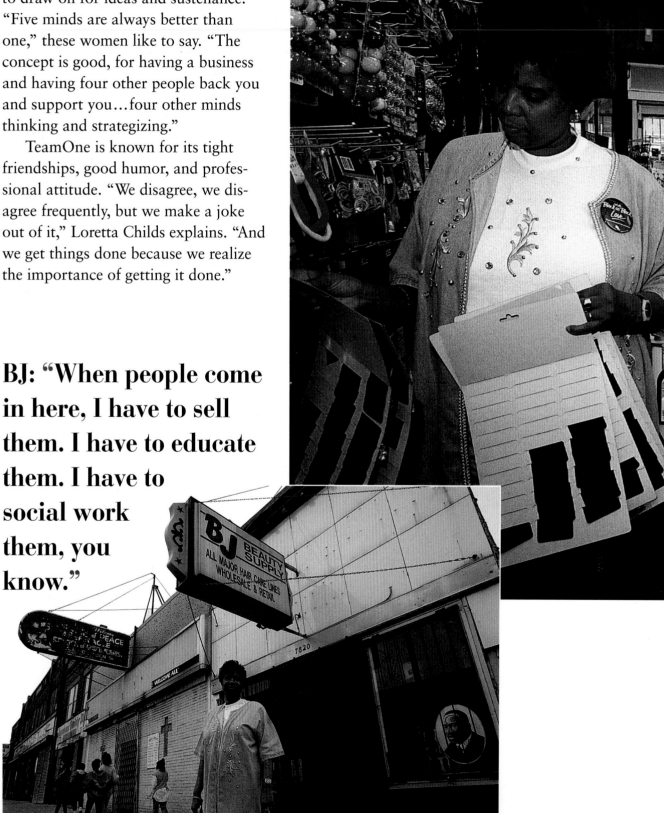

Way to Live."—Joseph Bruchac

"I'm going to help you do this. I'll show you how I work it and then maybe you can try it on your own next time."

Slay says, "When I'm doing my projects, it's their arms and legs that put it together. Loretta writes something. Sandy critiques it. Lillian does the artistic touch.... And Dorothy does our hair. They really have been a great help to me."

"Some girls," BJ Slay muses, "have some dreams right now. And they are a little bit hesitant to just start out here, and not have the money to support their dream."

"When time comes for these loans and you do have to put these packages together, it's hours you have to stand. . . . We might be up here till three o'clock in the morning sometimes."

—DOROTHY, WHO OPERATES A HAIRDRESSING BUSINESS FROM THE BACK OF SLAY'S STORE, PURCHASED THE EQUIPMENT WITH A WSEP LOAN.

"We were all pretty much called by BJ.... I can honestly say in lending support for one person," says hairdresser Dorothy, "I am helping myself to grow too."

If small business is the backbone of the economy, Women's Self-Employment Project members—including the Full Circle Fund—are improving its posture in Chicago. Their businesses include flower arranging and making dresses, dolls, and ethnic jewelry.

"A lot of these women are very creative; they had to become very creative because the majority of home-based businesses are born out of survival," says Colette Grant, WSEP member. And they are good money managers because they have learned to manipulate small funds to make it day by day. When they start their own businesses, according to Deborah Payne, another WSEP member, "It isn't work. And it isn't just money. It's self-expression, the

Chicago Spirit Award winners: The "Ladies of Success" circle helped Jewell Pates (far left) get the confidence to sell her products.

"I always did very creative things, but my weakness was that I didn't like to sell my products," Pates says. Thanks to a WSEP loan, Pates has become a successful businesswoman.

greatest luxury a working person can hope for."

"The group format for lending is really important," says Connie Evans of WSEP. Peer support breaks through the isolation the poor woman may feel; and peer pressure helps get the loans paid back on time.

"It's helping people use their own talents and skills," says Evans. "It's not just talking about debt and credit and capital, it's talking about building capital, building assets, and that's what's really important if we are going to take people from poverty."

The Full Circle Fund (WSEP), which is modeled on the Grameen Bank in Bangladesh and has inspired several hundred similar programs in the U.S., decided in 1986 to focus on women, the poorest of the poor, those with least access to capital for development, because they felt that if they could impact women they would impact children. Some successes: people starting a small business and getting off of public aid—their children are going to college and can help with some expenses now.

Self-employment, micro-enterprises, often started up for as little as $1,500, operated out of the home—these are some of the alternatives that have worked for women in Chicago.

Credit and collateral are major issues for people with very low incomes. Full Circle Fund launches its businesses by providing character-based lending; it follows up by offering a six-week training session on everything from self-esteem to basic bookkeeping.

Lending circles meet regularly every two weeks to make payments, brainstorm, discuss business plans, provide support. All loan decisions are put to a vote.

"When people have money and income they can exercise choice, which means they can participate in a democratic process," says WSEP's Connie Evans. "We are trying to bring people into an economic arena where hopefully they can play a larger role...because they now have access to resources.

"When women come together and they're helping each other on business issues, they begin to take on broader issues that affect the whole community.... They're taking on some kind of democratic process and institution building."

To every thing there is a season...
hope grows in a community

Love and the desire to help others. One person's passionate commitment to a project can nourish community hopes and help that community grow strong.

When Robert Moody's son Russell suffered a head injury in an auto accident, Robert was determined to make every effort to help the college-age boy rebuild his shattered life.

Robert's personal search for ways to help his son—in which he investigated physical therapy programs in the United States and abroad—led him to build innovative therapy facilities in his hometown of Galveston, Texas. One of the Moody Foundation's first projects was a transitional learning community (TLC), a program that provides a year of intensive therapy for people with head injuries.

His son, who was in a coma for months after his accident and, as his brother Ross describes it, in a "vegetative state" for years, entered the TLC program.

"The program taught Russell how to walk," Ross says. "It gave him extensive speech therapy, plus all different kinds of therapy and counseling.

"He came out a different person. Since that time he's lived by himself. He's married. He's working.

"It's the difference between night and day."

But Robert Moody, according to Sherry Kirwin, a therapy assistant, "didn't develop this program for Russell specifically. He developed the program for people that may have found themselves in Russell's situation."

So the Moody Foundation's programs have been Hope Therapy for many people, other families who have traveled from all over Texas to obtain rehabilitation and job training, and a special quality of care.

And the benefits of the Moody family's dedication and caring have spiraled out from the rehabilitation center and into the surrounding community.

"Wonderful hands-on people" is how Ross Moody describes the team of therapists who do hippotherapy in Hope Arena. "Moody Gardens' whole philosophy," says therapy assistant Sherry Kirwin, "is to make the world a better place and allow the same opportunities for all individuals in the world.... The Gardens provide the opportunity for individuals that may need special consideration in order to work here, or may need some special training, or have special needs in the way of rehabilitation."

"If you've always been in a wheelchair,
just imagine the boost you get sitting
high up on a horse."

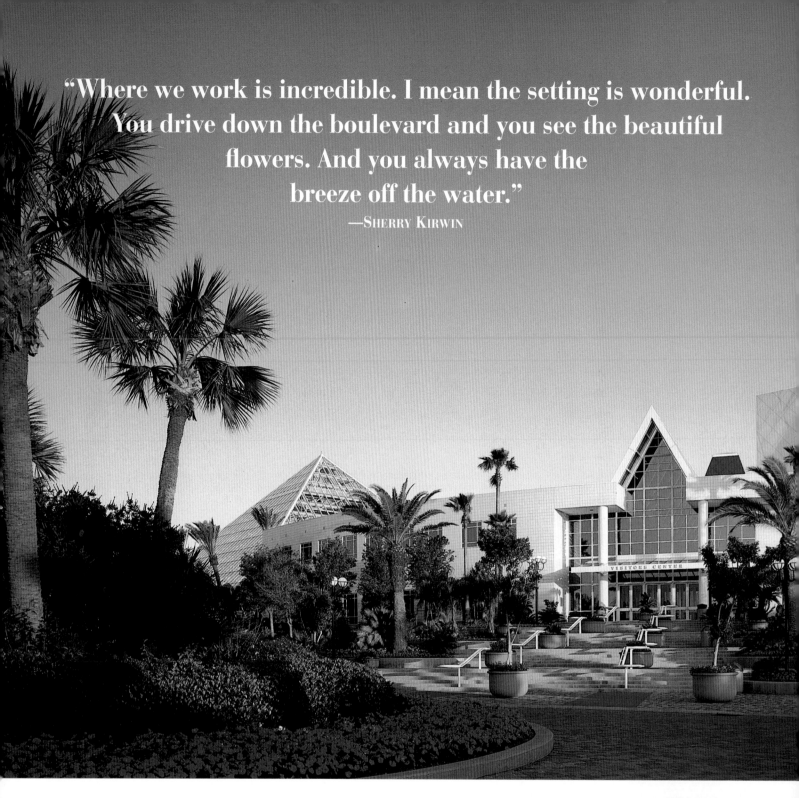

"Where we work is incredible. I mean the setting is wonderful. You drive down the boulevard and you see the beautiful flowers. And you always have the breeze off the water."
—SHERRY KIRWIN

Moody Gardens—a 142-acre former marsh near the Galveston airport—is a unique commercial venture. One million tourists visit the Gardens annually, whether to see an IMAX movie, tour the rainforest, swim at the adjacent Palm Beach, or see and pet exotic animals at the Gardens' Learning Place.

The other side of the venture offers unconditional love to the disabled: a paranoid schizophrenic learning to give a dog a bath; a severely burned child learning to touch again by brushing the soft fur of a chinchilla; a Down's Syndrome woman caring for seedlings that she is growing herself.

"Think about the psychological boost they're getting. The best thing about horseback riding is that they can control their environment."

Hope Therapy is a center for interactive therapy—employing a team of therapists. Today the rehab center offers riding therapy, animal-assisted therapy, horticultural therapy—all based on "the healing energy of interacting with living things."

But it started simply. After his son was injured, Robert Moody developed the idea of a rehabilitative riding program. The program started with two horses, a riding therapy assistant, and Sherry Kirwin.

Kirwin had a brother who needed therapy: he was in a cast up to his hips. The boy had been training a colt when injured.

Her family, she says, knew that "horses were a real motivator in the rehab process. We had used it at our barn." The boy had been able to train the horse from his wheelchair, eventually sliding onto the horse to continue the training.

The Moody Foundation had already built an arena, which was used for hippotherapy during the day and rented to circuses and rodeos at night.

Kirwin, a licensed therapist, got the handicapped riding program accredited, found additional gentle horses, and developed the new program's lesson plans.

About the program's benefits for the disabled, she says, "Think about the psychological boost they're getting. The best thing about horseback riding is that they can control their environment."

The gait of a horse, moreover, simulates the gait of a human, "the physical action of going riding helps people use their legs and gain balance." Therapists also encourage the practice of fine-motor skills "so that the kids don't realize they're working. For example, we might put rings on the horses' ears and then the child has to reach forward to get them off."

There are other good lessons, Kirwin says. "The opportunities are grand" to teach language. Kids discover what Kirwin calls "purposeful communication" when they stand up and tell their horse to "Go." And it mosies right along.

The program grew from just a few clients a week to as many as 90 people a week in the riding program, and 200 a week in animal-assisted therapy.

"We've got kids as young as 2 and our oldest client is in the 80s," Kirwin says. "As far as their disabilities, we've had neurological impairment, post-stroke, traumatic brain injury, kids with learning disabilities and Downs syndrome."

The Americans with Disabilities Act gave the disabled civil rights. Rehabilitation centers like Moody Gardens, says Kirwin, give them the training and opportunity to "live normal happy lives within their community."

Moody Gardens therapists take a hands-on approach to helping.

. . . a time to weep and a time to laugh . . .

"**When the hippotherapy program started working for Russell, people actually came looking to my dad for help for their family and for their friends and through that he realized that what he was doing for his son could be done for other people with similar situations.**" —Ross Moody

Galveston, home to Moody Gardens, is a fairly small town, some 62,000 people. It is not too surprising that a rehabilitation facility like the Moody Foundation has had an impact on the community. It has made residents of Galveston aware of people with disabilities and their needs.

The city established a coalition for barrier-free living in 1989. The same year, the community was surveyed to find out what percent of the population was disabled. The 11% figure turned out to be close to the national average of 10%; nonetheless, the city has been especially receptive to education programs and has made changes needed to bring the community into compliance with the Americans with Disabilities Act.

Hope Therapy charges only a nominal fee for its services, even subsidizing some care. To keep the project alive, Robert Moody capitalized on Galveston's draw as a tourist attraction. Eighty percent of Galveston Island's revenue is based on tourism, mainly visits to its historic homes and white sand beaches.

Moody built the Gardens as an additional tourist attraction for the community. Its theater, restaurant, convention center, rain forest pyramid—besides being a beautiful addition to the city—employ several hundred people. "Moody Gardens has evolved into a major presence in the community," says Ross Moody. Which, in turn, has caused an evolution in the Hope Therapy programs.

One day Sherry Kirwin looked around the botanical garden and real-

A ten-story glass rainforest pyramid, with a one-acre tropical ecosystem: pools, waterfalls, birds, butterflies. Tropical fish aquariums hold Motora rays, tricolor sharks, Frenatus eels, and more. There are strange animals: bird-eating spiders and poison-arrow frogs, among them. Medicinal plant projects carry on research in tropical plant uses and pharmacology. The Gardens' beneficial insects programs allows the pyramid plants to grow pesticide-free.

Moody Gardens also collaborates with Houston's Rainforest Action Group to do rainforest education in Galveston area schools.

ized "we were sitting in this tropical paradise of plants and plant material. So we started the horticultural therapy program." That was the beginning of the Gardens' vocational program.

"We started working with people with disabilities who were interested in gardening. They come here and learn gardening skills. And as Moody Gardens grew"—with fruit, vegetable, and herb gardens—"the job opportunities grew from that."

It is the interrelationship of educational, recreational, and therapeutic functions that gives Moody Gardens its vitality. As the Moody Foundation motto says, "Created to help people with special needs, Moody Gardens continues to enlighten and enrich us all."

We're All in This Together

COMMON GROUND: where varying interests come together. When individuals become isolated and apathetic, they cease to participate as part of a group. They become, at best, cogs in a machine. But political or social action—getting things done—always occurs within the context of a *community*. We band together with neighbors to fix the street or raise money for playground equipment or close down a crackhouse. That is why grass-roots activity is often more effective than top-down political action, for it is at the grass-roots level that community ties are usually the strongest.

The key challenge, then, is to find *common ground:* "This land is my land, this land is your land."

Both the word *common* and the word *community* derive from the Latin roots *com* (together) and *unus* (one). Come together. *"E pluribus unum."*

Common ground refers to what is *common* to a *community.* Since the fourteenth century, the notion of community, of the commons, has been applied to the *people* as distinguished from an elite. "We, the people."

Finding *common ground* means finding what is inclusive rather than exclusive. The existence of public life and democratic politics depends on our ability to share the public square —the *commons*—and to seek out and value what we hold as one, to make decisions that will serve us all. Working together to solve problems: this is the essence and the genius of the democratic process.

**Pitching in:
In a circus community,
all sorts of people share a
common purpose and work
together for the good
of the group.**

167

Common ground: "the place where . . .

Finding common ground can mean the survival of a society. Especially if the dispute is over water—and the nature of America's future.

Renee Askins, head of the Wolf Fund, is both biologist and political activist. The view of common ground she developed through her work is mystical, ecological—and very practical.

To her mind, "Common ground is the place where the either/or doesn't exist. Where it is not us against them.

"It is not," she explains, "environmentalists against ranchers, hunters against animal rights [activists], wolves against livestock. It is the place where there is room for all of those things."

But in an overcrowded world, there seems to be less room for all things—and first to be jettisoned may be the wilderness values that have been close to the hearts of Americans since the nation's founding.

The fight for the wildness that is "the preservation of all things" is currently raging on the riverbanks of California's Sierra Nevadas and in its fertile Sacramento Delta. The dispute is over the fate of the American River—and the question of how to balance the needs of man and the rest of the natural world.

After years of arguing about the river's future, four of the community's most fervent disputants decided to search for Askins's common ground: "the place where we bring honor and respect for other points of view and other values."

The place they chose for their searching was the beautiful canyon of the upper American River. Together they rafted

we bring honor and respect for . . .

down the river, through difficult whitewater in the heaviest spring runoff in years.

Running the rapids is the kind of experience that might lead to compromise—"different values coming together," in Askins's definition, "and shifting and moving to make room for each other."

The opponents in this dispute over water use were "all in the same boat." Living out this realization, negotiating the river together—how did this bring them closer to an understanding of their community's needs?

AS THEY TRAVELED DOWN the American River, four men in a raft—plus a female river guide—continued a debate that had been going on for years. It is the kind of debate over water use and future generations that is going on all over America.

They argued about controlling the river, about proposals for a federal project, the Auburn Dam. The most ambitious plan calls for a billion-dollar dam that would provide flood control to the Sacramento floodplain in wet years, water storage in dry years, and hydroelectric power year round.

A mammoth project, the proposed dam would put 48 miles of pristine canyon along the river under water, eliminating acres of forest, sand and gravel bars, and many lovely riverside trails.

Dam opponents argue for river preservation and a more conservative style of water management. They want to repair the existing Folsom Dam and the area's network of levees and also create underground water storage for dry years.

Their conservatism is in line with water policy change nationwide. The U.S. Bureau of Reclamation, which built dams all over the West in past decades, now sees its role more as

Although you could describe their positions as pro- or anti-dam, during their raft trip down the American River, Bruce Cosgrove and David Breninger (pro) and Gary Estes and Bill Center (anti) expressed all facets of the debate over water use taking place across America today.

In the tumbling raft, their voices merge against the roar of the river rapids. They argue that "the people in this boat and the people we represent have the ability to come up with a solution."

Decisions on "this most complicated public policy problem" must be made by people who are less "interested in winning than in succeeding—meeting the needs that have driven the debate over the dam."

They talk about "interest-based bargaining" and balancing the demands of farmers, industry, tourism, property owners, developers, and conservationists.

They talk about economic needs—and basic spiritual needs, "the greater community good."

Says one of the men, "Something that I think has been overlooked in all this is the community that can't speak.

"We're surrounded by it. Whether it be this little stone outcropping, whether it be the trees, the life here.

"That's a value that exists whether people see it or don't see it. And how does that get cranked into the cost-benefit analysis?"

. . . other points of view and other values."

"resource manager—a protective organization, as opposed to a development organization."

According to a *National Geographic* Special Edition on "Water in North America," even the U. S. Army Corps of Engineers, which once touted the development that dams brought to a region, is now willing to admit that "the side effects can be devastating."

"A river is essentially transmitting life," explains conservationist Kevin J. Coyle, president of the American Rivers Group. "It's moving life from one place to another. These blockages stop that transmission. They shut down the systems, killing them off. It's a chain reaction of death."

It is truly a life-and-death matter, our debate over water. As communities grow, there is an increasing demand for more water, more power, more flood control, and more recreational uses. As populations grow, water is pumped out of existing aquifers to grow crops and provide water to cities. "The time will come," Thomas Merton predicted, "when they will sell you even your rain." Yet water is the earth's most "common ground." It covers three-quarters of the earth's surface. It is also our own "common ground"—the human body is two-thirds water. Water is the source of life itself, and it is the most critical substance for sustaining life. It is a community trust.

In preserving water, we preserve ourselves.

"Democracy is the art of running the

Democracy works when we respect one another's individuality as we strive to find common ground. Today, new bioregional voices are calling for a greater sense of place, which is one approach to establishing shared values. But Laura Nader, an anthropologist at the University of California, Berkeley, has pointed out that finding common ground depends above all else upon sharing a common purpose. In this there is promise for a mobile society.

To really appreciate a common purpose, try traveling with the Kelly Miller Circus. For most of the year many of the residents of the town of Hugo, Oklahoma, hit the road as modern-day nomads, taking their circus from town to town.

The enormous task of moving a small city and entertainment conglomerate is made simpler when the goal is shared and the motivation is universal.

ircus from the monkey cage." —H.L. Mencken

"Circus" means *circle:* The word refers to the circular riding ring of the show's equestrian origins. Circus performances occur in rings inside circular tents, as the audience circles around to watch in wonder. Acrobats and animals delight us with hoops and rings. In this the circus is a metaphor for life, which is part of the appeal of the circus. All of us live within circles of nature and community.

Finding common ground can be quite a balancing act.

Clowns, barkers, animal trainers, high-wire artists, electricians, managers—a community can hardly get more diverse. Yet all work together, pulling up stakes and putting them down again at hundreds of one-night stands a season. It costs tens of thousands of dollars a day to put on a circus show, and everyone has a job to do. The welfare of the entire community depends on the efforts of each one of its members

With this kind of experience, it is not surprising that Hugo's mayor David E. Rawls (a veteran circus performer and manager) understands that participation and consensus are keys not only to putting on a successful circus but also to building a healthy community.

Thanks to community activism, Hugo has become a Federal Enterprise Community. Today the town is hiring a city manager and planning a variety of new outreach and endeavor programs. This is one town that just keeps on moving.

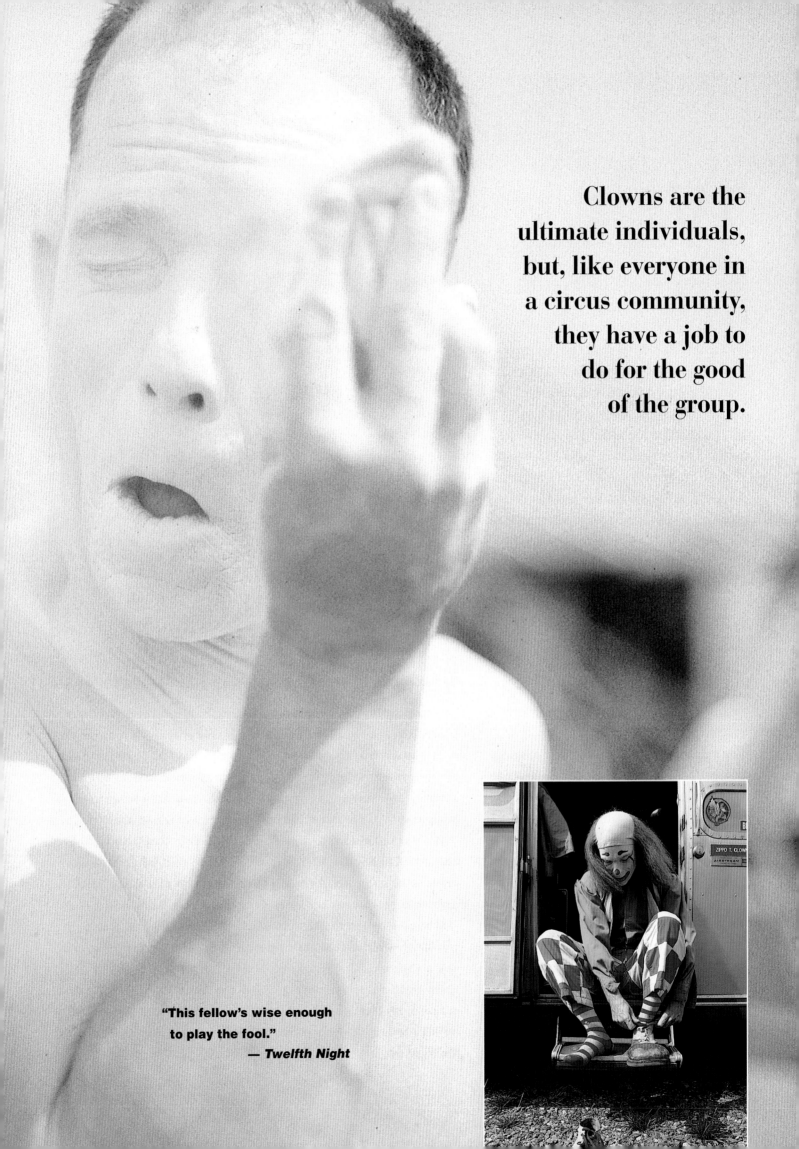

Clowns are the ultimate individuals, but, like everyone in a circus community, they have a job to do for the good of the group.

"This fellow's wise enough
to play the fool."
— *Twelfth Night*

W hen the founders spoke of "forging a democracy," the image was alive for them. Fire, hammer, iron—and the hand-made tools created thereby—were a part of their everyday lives.

Blacksmithing is a 3,000-year-old tradition. At the time of the American Revolution, the village blacksmith was central to his community, creating agri-cultural tools, kitchen implements.

Today, blacksmithing in America often combines utilitarian and artistic functions. Tom Joyce of Santa Fe, New Mexico, is one of America's best and youngest blacksmiths, a craftsman and an artist.

Speaking about his work in *THE* magazine, Joyce provided a model for thinking about the work of creating human society:

"Designing projects with subtle his-toric reference and offering multiple layers in which the pieces may be under-stood continue to be important criteria for my work. They not only build on the past's design vocabulary, but also assure an affirmative alliance between all work created by hand.

"Each human contribution to the arts has been developed through the investigation of others, and passed as gifts to their successors. Acknowledg-ing this credit to humanity's collabora-tion of sorts is necessary in providing another piece of our global view, so important to our future survival."

"Agricultural tools, such as a grubbing hoe, whose design has evolved over centuries of practical use, continue to inspire me," says blacksmith Tom Joyce. "Out of context, these tools are purely sculptural in form and design, and while in use, ab-solutely efficient and timeless in their connection to what is inseparable in our lives, family, thought, work, and play."

He learned his art by examining all the old tools, household hardware, and wrought-iron work he could find, often creating replicas of antiques, as he discovered which piece had "that in-definable yet necessary ingredient that made its design speak."

When he began to get commissions for architectural and art work, he retained this connection to the "vernacular" of every-day art forms.

Understanding the nature of fire and metal, the speed of the process, imitating early blacksmiths who "cranked [implements] out like breath," Joyce learned to exploit the "imperfections of his forgings."

old-fashioned art

"Struck with the hammer, the insensate ore has begun to sing."

Joyce's vision reveals the organic structure in hammered metal, forging links between form and ornamentation in his work.

The same sense of organic relationship and forged connections shapes his thinking about his role in his community. The way that his work reveals the forged connections, the unification of disparate parts, illuminates the meaning of community for him.

Santa Maria de la Paz is the first new church built in Santa Fe in 30 years. At the entrance to the church is a rough granite boulder that cradles a bronze and iron baptismal font that Joyce created. The font is a hammered and folded bronze bowl; surrounding it are iron pieces forged from donations of the parishioners. Forged from objects that had special meaning for the parishioners, the font has become a sort of parish reliquary. It holds holy water into which parishioners dip their fingers as they cross themselves each time they enter the church.

The story of the church and its members is preserved in the metal font, the interlocking pieces of their lives creating a vital design, with each piece representing "a memory, a piece of the past."

The granite block for the baptismal font cracked as it was being carved. "To pull together a solution for the problem of this cracked rock, without having to remove it," Joyce said, "I decided to work with the fabric of the lives of the community."

Parishioners donated 450 pounds of metal for Joyce to use in crafting a font for their church. "Donations," according to Edward Lebow of *American Craft Magazine*, "included bits of tire chains that once saved someone in a snowstorm, a nail found in Jerusalem by a nun, keys." Mementos and souvenirs, wagon parts, old tools, and baling wire.

"Sacred power means reality." —Mircea Eliade

In the matrix of the community a new generation enters life. At the church's font, the community welcomes a new member, with name and saving grace.

Joyce's work will mark the passage of time. The bronze bowl of the baptismal font is intended to change color as it ages. Eventually, the water will stain the granite rock as it drips over it. The font will achieve "a historical presence."

Art and community: this is the richness, the variety and subtlety of Joyce's organic vision.

In Joyce's words about fine metal, "Up close it was as imperfect as life." His work celebrates "humanity's collaboration" as it forges a joyous link between past and future.

When the font was consecrated, Joyce says, "it brought tears to my eyes, to witness something that really created a sacred space."

"All work produced through thoughtful, caring purpose will speak to us, teach us, and be completely approachable, even if not completely understandable. Whether it is functional or not, craft or art, it is all inseparable and indecipherable when created with an impassioned honesty."

New Mexico's traditional farms. . .

A ribbon of water holds many New Mexico communities together through spring flood and summer drought.

Acequias are loops of water that feed out of a river, meander through farm fields, and return to the river. A circle of community shares the precious water.

The cooperative associations that manage these "mother ditches" have endured for hundreds of years. Year after year, residents gather to maintain age-old waterways, friends and neighbors working side by side to keep the water flowing.

The acequia—both the irrigation ditch and the association of water users—has long been the social, economic, and political core of village life.

The acequia system combines Spanish and Indian irrigation methods. When the Spanish arrived in New Mexico, the Indians had already built dams and canals to carry water to fields.

In Spanish law, land and water rights are inseparable, and acequias to cultivate village fields were often dug before the land was cleared or any houses were built.

Canoas are hollowed-out logs that carry water over arroyos. Early settlers made these flumes by hollowing out the tall straight pine trees that grew along nearby slopes. Stone dams divert water. Wooden headgates control the flow of water through a network of ditches. When the headgate is opened, the mayordomo walks the water down through the ditch, accompanying it as it moves slowly along the ancient course.

The building of the acequia, according to member Max Córdova of Truchas, "reveals the intimate relationship our ancestors had with this land," the place that they settled between the 16th and the 18th century.

In a masterpiece of sensitive engineering, acequia builders followed the natural water courses down the mountain slopes, adjusting their paths for trees and boulders. Digging the ditches by hand with wooden spades and knives and transporting the soil on rawhide slings, the earliest Spanish settlers added miles of irrigation ditches to the Indian canals they had found in New Mexico.

Top: Shareholder Ernesto Montoya (left) with his uncle Tomás Montoya. Below: Tomás finds his father's name on the original acequia agreement, from a century ago.

provide a pattern for community living. Fields

The acequia is run democratically—each farmer owns one water share and has one vote in the annual meeting at which water rates and rations are set. The ditch is governed by a *mayordomo* and a commission of three landowners, all of whom are elected. "But the commission," according to Geoff Bryce, a member of the Taos Valley Acequia Commission, "doesn't really take any action without knowing it's the consensus of the community."

The mayordomo is paid a monthly salary to organize work crews for the annual cleaning and other needed repairs, to watch the ditch for overflow or blockage, and to collect water fees.

There are customs and duties that form the cooperative community of the acequia. The annual cleaning is one of these. A shareholder can pay $25 to avoid his duty, but, as one farmer says, "you care about your neighbors," so you do the work yourself instead. First, the new growth in the ditch is pruned back. Then a party of as many as 100 people assemble on the banks of the acequia

Cleaning the ditches: "Their grassy banks must be dug back each year and trimmed of last season's growth of willow canes and cottonwood suckers, plum and bush cherry, and the silt and sand and dead leaves scraped off the bottom in order to receive the first water." —Stanley Crawford, *A Garlic Testament*

with picks and shovels to clean the ditch of silt, section by section, with the work group moving slowly along the entire length of the ditch, repairing the banks as they go.

"I don't know any other community effort like this one in the entire country," says Stanley Crawford, author of *Mayordomo,* which he wrote after participating in an acequia association. "People working together two or three days at a time."

Public responsibility is as much the lifeblood of the community as the water it shares.

Eight hundred to twelve hundred acequias deliver water to a patchwork of small farms dotting rural New Mexico. Land holdings tend to be small: water is used for orchards and truck farms, most less than 20 acres, for kitchen gardens and stock raising. Garlic, onions, peppers, squash, corn, beans, lettuce—all are carefully cultivated with shared water.

where democracy works as the land is worked.

"There are places in the acequia where I can just lay down, put my hands in the water, and drink out of the acequia." —ERNESTO MONTOYA

"The acequia is a reason to come together, to co-operate. People don't have to like each other, but they have to know each other, and to work together."
—MAYORDOMO STANLEY CRAWFORD

For the Amish labor is a product not an expense. In the sense that community labor produces community, acequia laborers also bear witness to this view.

"The best man is like water." —LAO TZU

"I know where most of the weak spots are in the bank and where they will have to be built up and where the grass has grown constrictlingly thick and where the channel must be widened a little, and there will be enough sandbars to shovel out on the inside of bends on the serpentine course: this will be the work that proves enough to tire my workers by the end of the day. And almost any-thing we do will serve to keep the ditch wide and deep enough to accept the rolling tongue of water, clogged with leaves and twigs, muddy and white foamed, that will race down the three-foot-wide channel two days from now." —Stanley Crawford, *Mayordomo*

A shareholder in the acequia is considered a steward of land and water. A modern conception of water as a commodity to be bought and sold has created what Crawford calls "a clash of ideas and purpose."

Geoff Bryce says, "In the western United States, we've come up against a limit to growth and the limit to growth is water. Water was never a market commodity before, but it is now."

When an acequia shareholder retires or sells his land and water claim, there is one less member to maintain the acequia, and, as Crawford says, "one more piece of the community lost forever."

There is another challenge facing the Truchas acequia. Citing low turnout at an annual cleaning, the U.S. Army Corps of Engineers has proposed an easement through wilderness area to install a 1.6–mile PVC plastic pipe tunnel.

It is an expensive project and one that could destroy the centuries-old cooperative system of villagers. In the new system a farmer would need cash instead of labor to obtain water; this would ruin many of the poorer farmers.

Land use is already changing as younger New Mexicans move away to jobs and cities.

Small farmer Crawford observes in his book *A Garlic Testament:* "The rest of the world is always there, just outside the gate. Now and then it must be heeded. It must be attended to, studied, fretted over.

"And taking your goods to market and selling them is a way to discover just what is out there—even at times what you can do about it—to hold your streams and woods, your ditches and fields, your patch of garlic safe against the city's long-range plans, its schemes for becoming bigger and more powerful and farther-reaching."

AUGUSTINE ATILANO:

"Water flowing in the acequia is like wind blowing in the trees, blood flowing in your body. There is life in the water."

The "Song of the Acequias"—fingers of water bring life to an arid valley.

"If the water ceases to flow in our acequia systems," says Ernesto Montoya, "the land itself will die."

"We need to have the maintenance," he says. "We need to have the continuation of the cultural and the historical and all the values of the acequias, to have them continue for our children throughout the land."

"Generations through generations," says Montoya, "it's been going on. And we mean to keep it going for generations to come.

"God gave us this good land of ours and I think he gave it to us to respect and to cherish and to treat it religiously and to treat it right."

Of the community values created by the acequias, they say, "It was a way of life and it's still a way of life. It's something that can make people work together in harmony."

SAYS ONE TAOS RESIDENT:

"I see the acequia system as working very well in a democratic way, where we all have a common goal and a common need and we work together to achieve that need."

AFTERWORD

Finding a Public Voice
by Maxine Hong Kingston

CENTER ON PEOPLE. That is the message of living and of a living democracy. And it is the message of this book.

As a writer I have been immeasurably blessed by all of the people I've worked with. They have inspired and heartened me. I love to write-in-community. Writing-in-community with a group of men and women, I harness the energy, the atmosphere of the group to write more and well.

For the past several years I have worked with the Community of Mindful Living in Berkeley, California, giving writing workshops to war veterans. My work with combat veterans affirms some ideas I've been contemplating in my newest book, entitled *The Fifth Book of Peace*. Knowing war, virtually all of the veterans are pacifists.

In the writing and meditation workshops, 30 men and women who have been traumatized by their war experiences tell about their lives, listen, respond to one another, and transform their lives and mine. The purpose of these workshops is to write and reflect on one's life and experiences, and thus bring healing to the wounds of war, suffering, and social injustice.

Many veterans have described to me "coming of age" by writing letters home from war. Writing has been their main way to learn about themselves, and to make sense of their lives. By listening, they let the stories of others come into their bodies and hearts. We help one another carry the stories.

We learn and grow and heal by studying feelings and powerful events, working with memories. We need to define ourselves and our history, work out the values that give strength to our life. It is those values that allow us to "come home," to find the health, wholeness, and joy in our lives.

My books starting with *The Woman Warrior* have been about this process of understanding self so that one can act in the world. Find one's voice, and speak out in the world. There is an authoritative voice that emerges when one looks deeply at one's life.

Our immortality is to pass our stories on. As my co-teacher Larry Heinemann says, Pass the story on, tell it honestly, and let the listener and reader become responsible. The listener is your student, your child, your neighbor, your fellow worker—your community .

I have been teaching almost as long as I have been writing. For me, teaching writing is teaching living. The lessons are the same: Pay attention. Tell the truth. Learn to see. Learn to listen. Resolution of difficulties comes through hanging in there. As you write, listen, meditate, reflect, a compassionate understanding occurs.

The lessons for citizenship are lessons of individual engagement and participation in the building of a communal society. Dare to come to grips with the big themes in your life. Center on real things. Create yourself and become a strong person, and at the same time create a peaceful world.

Make sense of your experience. To learn what America's freedom of expression means, practice it. Strength comes from practice—and from values, the values so well stated in the Bill of Rights and the Five Wonderful Precepts of Buddhism.

A good democratic forum is a good spiritual forum—acting with compassion and appreciation for others. That is what this book celebrates.

Practice peace and heal the wounds of social injustice. With creative and spiritual insight and ideas of peace we can form blueprints for making America and the world anew.

ACKNOWLEDGMENTS

About the Author

James C. Crimmins is executive producer of *The American Promise* television series. He has produced numerous award-winning prime-time PBS series, including *American Enterprise*, *The Challenge of the Unknown*, and *The Search for Solutions*, which have been seen in classrooms by more than 400 million students. A former associate publisher of *Harper's* magazine, he is founder of the acclaimed *Business Times* television program.

EVERY PROJECT LIKE *The American Promise* involves hundreds of people who deserve praise and thanks. The series would not have been possible if it were not for the initial trust and support of Farmers Insurance Group of Companies, notably its Chairman, Leo Denlea, and Vice President of Corporate Communications, Jeffrey Beyer.

The struggle to find great stories that surprise and move us started some three years ago. The resulting content of the series is thanks to Deborah Hudson, her persistent team of researchers, and field producers Jeb Sharp, Toody Healy, Peter Powell, and Jonathan Halperin. Special thanks for the images on the screen are due to director of photography Robert Elfstrom and his crews—and a select list of top documentary camerapersons. Documentaries are usually made in the editing room; this one was certainly no exception, so special thanks are owed to Editor Jay Hansell and his associates Joe deFrancesco and David Schickele for their story-telling skills. Thanks to Tom Weidlinger and Allison Prince for the convincing historical sequences. The sound of the series is due to Ed Bogas a.k.a. "Quick Pencil," who gave the choral groups and musicians superb melodies to sing and play. Thanks are due John McCracken and John Vanore for producing the companion CD issued by Windham Hill (also thanks to Ann Robinson and Roy Gatinella of Windham Hill for enthusiastic support), and to arrangers Byron Olson and Moses Hogan; the Northwest Girlchoir, the St. Olaf Choir and the Moses Hogan Chorale, nearly 200 singers in all, for making the metaphor of democracy, different voices in harmony, move us as only music can. The series writing in tone, spirit, wit, and vibrancy is due to Deborah Hudson and Jeb Sharp. The narrator Joe Morton added his extraordinary

The logo for *The American Promise* television series was painted on a brick wall in the South Bronx by muralist Per-One, Alfredo Oyague.

talent to bind the series, all fifty-some stories, into a unified whole.

Thanks for this book go to Mark Powelson and Pamela Byers at KQED Books and Tapes and especially to Thomas and Carol Christensen, who took literally a library full of research, interviews, background information, production notes, transcripts, excerpts from advisor meetings, and our writing and assembled it with the help of Art Director Paula Schlosser into a book that is a delight to the eye and mind. Also thanks to a raft of photographers who captured vivid still images of our grass-roots adventure.

Thanks are due Mary Bitterman and Kevin Harris of KQED and to Ervin Duggan and the program team of PBS, whose parallel interest in democracy gave the series a superb launch. Their collective enthusiasm made all our tasks easier.

Special thanks from beginning to end of this project go to Suzanne Hogan for keeping the whole project in good spirits and on track and to Deborah Hudson for writing the verbal blueprint that gave the series an eloquent standard.

Certainly grateful applause is due to the hundreds of people, our citizen heroes, in the series who gave their time to make what is seen on screen and pictured in this book become a collective portrait of this country at its best. They are, as one of them said, "truly democracy in action."

Thanks go to a board of advisors who argued for and against approaches, ideas, stories, writing, scenes, whose involvement made sure the series properly represented the critical ideas and factors that make our democracy work.

Finally, I wish to thank my coast-to-coast family and especially my wife, Jennifer, for her patience and understanding lo these many months when deadlines and grass-roots democracy came into our lives. —JAMES C. CRIMMINS

BOARD OF ADVISORS

BENJAMIN BARBER
Director of the Walt Whitman Center for the Culture
    and Politics of Democracy
Rutgers University
New Brunswick, New Jersey

UNITA BLACKWELL
past Mayor of Mayersville, Mississippi
organizer of the Mississippi Freedom Democratic Party
former Vice-President of the National Conference of
    Black Mayors
Mayersville, Mississippi

ERNEST BOYER
President of the Carnegie Foundation for the
    Advancement of Teaching
Princeton, New Jersey

ALAN BULLOCK
former Vice Chancellor of Oxford University
Oxford University
St. Catherine's College
Oxford, England

JAMES FISHKIN
Darrell K. Royal Regents Chair in Ethics and
    American Society
Chair, Department of Government
University of Texas
Austin, Texas

LAWRENCE FRIEDMAN
Marion Rice Kirkwood Professor of Law
Stanford University Law School
Stanford, California

SHANTO IYENGAR
Professor of Political Science and Communication
    Studies
University of California
Los Angeles, California

KATHLEEN HALL JAMIESON
Professor and Dean of the Annenberg School for
    Communication
University of Pennsylvania
Philadelphia, Pennsylvania

DANIEL KEMMIS
Mayor of Missoula, Montana
author of *Community and the Politics of Place*
Missoula, Montana

GLENN LOURY
Professor of Economics
Boston University
Boston, Massachusetts

THEODORE LOWI
John L. Senior Professor of American Institutions
Government Department
Cornell University
Ithaca, New York

JANE MANSBRIDGE
Professor of Political Science
Faculty of the Center for Urban Affairs and Policy
    Research
Northwestern University
Evanston, Illinois

MARGIT MCGUIRE
former President of the National Council for the
    Social Studies
Chair, Teacher Education Program and Professor of
    Education
Seattle University
Seattle, Washington

DOUGLAS MILLER
High School Teacher
Department Chair of Social Studies
Fremont High School
Sunnyvale, California

LAURA NADER
Professor of Anthropology
University of California, Berkeley
Berkeley, California

DOUGLASS NORTH
1993 Nobel Prize Laureate in Economics
Professor of Economics
Washington University
St. Louis, Missouri

GEORGE PRIEST
John M. Olin Professor of Law and Economics
Yale Law School
New Haven, Connecticut

ROBERT PUTNAM
Clarence Dillon Professor of International Affairs
Center for International Affairs
Harvard University
Cambridge, Massachusetts

Denny Schillings
current President of the National Council for the
    Social Studies
High School Teacher
Homewood-Flossmoor High School
Homewood, Illinois

Raymond Shonholtz
Founder of Community Boards
President, Partners for Democratic Change
San Francisco, California

Lawrence Susskind
Associate Director of the Program on Negotiation at
    Harvard Law School
Professor of Urban Studies and Planning
Massachusetts Institute of Technology
Cambridge, Massachusetts

Selected Advisor Readings

Barber, Benjamin R. "Rights and Democracy: The Reconstruction of Rights," in *Current*, no. 335, Sept. 1991.

_____. *Strong Democracy* (Berkeley: University of California 1984).

_____, and Watson, Patrick. *The Struggle for Democracy* (Boston: Little, Brown & Co. 1989).

Fishkin, James S. *Democracy and Deliberation: New Directions for Democratic Reform* (New Haven: Yale University Press, 1991).

Friedman, Lawrence M. *The Republic of Choice: Law, Authority, and Culture* (Cambridge: Harvard University Press, 1990).

Iyengar, Shanto. *News that Matters* (Chicago: University of Chicago Press, 1987).

Jamieson, Kathleen Hall. *Dirty Politics: Deception, Distraction, and Democracy* (New York: Oxford University Press, 1992).

Kemmis, Daniel. *Community and the Politics of Place* (Norman, OK: University of Oklahoma Press, 1990).

_____. *The Good City and the Good Life* (Boston: Houghton Mifflin, 1995).

Loury, Glenn C. *One by One, From the Inside Out: Essays and Reviews on Race and Responsibility in America.* (New York: Free Press, 1995).

Lowi, Theodore J. *American Government: Freedom and Power.* (New York: Norton, 1990).

McGuire, Margit E. "Whose Voices Will Be Heard? Creating a Vision for the Future," in *Social Education* (vol. 56, no. 2, 1992).

Mansbridge, Jane J. *Beyond Adversary Democracy* (Chicago: University of Chicago Press, 1983).

North, Douglass C. *Institutions, Institutional Change and Economic Performance* (Cambridge: Cambridge University Press, 1990).

Putnam, Robert D. *Making Democracy Work: Civic Traditions in Modern Italy* (Princeton: Princeton University Press, 1992).

———. "Bowling Alone: America's Declining Social Capital," in *Journal of Democracy*, vol. 6, no. 1, Jan. 1995.

———. "The Prosperous Community: Social Capital and Public Life," in *The American Prospect*, no. 13, Spring 1993.

Schillings, Denny L. *The Living Constitution.* (New York: McGraw-Hill, 1991).

Susskind, Lawrence E. *Environmental Diplomacy: Negotiating More Effective Agreements.* Oxford: Oxford University Press, 1994).

SOURCES

"... to be shaping again, model
and tool, craft of culture,
how we go on."
— Gary Snyder, "Axe Handles"

PHOTOGRAPHY CREDITS

The sources for the photos appearing in this book are listed below. Credits for the photographers are listed by page number in sequence with successive pages indicated by hyphens; where necessary, the positions of the photos are indicated, separated from the page numbers with parentheses.

© Nita Winter: xxvi, 30, 86, 87, 94 (top), 116 (right)

Peter Ralston: 3, 12

Ferne Pearlstein: front cover, 4–5, 16–23, 66–69, 74–75 (right), 76 (left), 78, 79 (top right, center right, bottom)–83, 84 (center, bottom)–85, 88–91, 106, 108– 111, 115–116 (top left), 117–119 (left), 126, 128–129, 134 (center left, bottom right), 136–137, 139 (top right), 145, 166–167, 170–175, 183–184, 186 (bottom)–187

Andrew Eccles: 6, 33 (bottom), 34 (bottom), 35 (bottom left, right)–38, 72, 150–152, 161, 164–165 (top), 168, 176–182, 185–186 (top), 188–189

© Jeff Dwarsky: 8–11, 13 (bottom)–15

© Rob Badger: 24–25 (left), 95, 132–133, 134–135 (background), 136 (top)

© Renee Lynn: 25 (right), 26–27

© Tom Mareschal/The Image Bank, © 1995: 28–29

© Gil Barerra: 32–33 (left), 35 (top left), 39

George Herben/Alaska Stock Images, © 1995: 40 (left)

Clark Mishler/Alaska Stock Images, © 1995: iv, 40 (right)–42

Chris Arend/Alaska Stock Images, © 1995: 43–44

© Jeb Sharp, 45

Rick Tully: 46–47

© Bill Ellzey: 48–49, 64–65

Arlene Gottfried: front cover, iii, xxiv–xxv, 50, 92, 127, 130, 146–147, 154–158

© Gus Powell: 51, 53 (bottom), 54 (top)

© Porter Gifford: 52–53 (top), 54 (bottom)–57

Chris Shorten: front cover, vii, xii, 58–63

© Harriet Zucker/photonica: 70

Charles Place/The Image Bank, © 1995: 73

Greg Mironchuck: 75

David Barry: 76 (right), 79 (top left), 140–143

Reprinted by permission of the publisher from Jack Gannon, *The Week the World Heard Gallaudet.* Washington, DC, (Gallaudet University Press., 1989) © 1989 by Gallaudet University: 84 (top)

World Wide Photo: 94 (bottom)

Kevin R. Wolf: 96–97

Charlotte *Observer:* 98–100

Pacific News Service/YO: 101

Larry Dale/The Image Bank, © 1995: 102–103 (background)

City of Santa Monica: 103

L. Barry Hetherington: 104

Marvin E. Newman/The Image Bank, © 1995: 105

YES!: 107

Eric Tadsen: 112–113

Knoxville *News Sentinel:* 119 (lower right)

Ted Wood Photography: 120

Yellowstone National Park: 121, 122 (right)–123

LuRay Parker, Wyoming Game and Fish: 122 (left)

John Morrison/photonica: 124

San Francisco *Chronicle,* Deanne Fitzmaurice: 138 (top)–139

San Francisco Examiner, Kurt Rogers: 148

Joe Aker Photography: 162 (top)

Moody Gardens: 162 (bottom)–163, 165 (bottom)

The Chicago *Defender:* 159

Catherine Nance: 193